PENGUIN BOOKS
100 LYRICS

One of India's most respected film-makers, Gulzar has directed some of the enduring classics of Hindi cinema like *Parichay*, *Mausam*, *Aandhi*, *Angoor*, *Ijaazat* and *Maachis*, remembered not only for their storytelling but also their unforgettable songs. He continues to be one of the most popular lyricists in mainstream Hindi cinema with several recent chartbusters to his credit.

Apart from the many Filmfare and National Awards for his films and lyrics, Gulzar has also received the Sahitya Akademi Award in 2002 and the Padma Bhushan in 2004. In 2009 he became the first Indian lyricist to win an Oscar for the song '*Jai ho*' from the film *Slumdog Millionaire*; the song went on to win a Grammy in 2010. Gulzar lives and works in Mumbai.

Sunjoy Shekhar was born in Sahebganj, a sleepy town on the banks of the Ganga where part of *Bandini*, the motion picture for which Gulzar wrote his first song, was filmed. Sunjoy tells stories for a living, and has more than three thousand hours of story-writing credits on a host of television channels across India and Indonesia. He divides his time between Mumbai, New Delhi and Jakarta.

100 Lyrics

GULZAR

Translated by
SUNJOY SHEKHAR

PENGUIN BOOKS

PENGUIN BOOKS

USA | Canada | UK | Ireland | Australia
New Zealand | India | South Africa | China

Penguin Books is part of the Penguin Random House group of companies
whose addresses can be found at global.penguinrandomhouse.com

Published by Penguin Random House India Pvt. Ltd
7th Floor, Infinity Tower C, DLF Cyber City,
Gurgaon 122 002, Haryana, India

Penguin
Random House
India

First published in Viking by Penguin Books India 2009

Published in Penguin Books 2012

Copyright © Gulzar 2009

Translation copyright © Sunjoy Shekhar 2009

All rights reserved

10 9 8 7 6 5 4 3 2

ISBN 9780143418207

Typeset in Sabon by Eleven Arts
Printed at Repro Knowledgecast Limited, India

www.penguin.co.in

Forenote

The celebrated popular musician Sting inspired me to compile this book. I have published several volumes of my poetry before, and compiled my lyrics separately in two small volumes in Hindi. Somehow I didn't mix the two, except when my poems were picked up for a film, and dressed up with a musical rendering.

Sting in his book of lyrics used an interesting analogy in the introduction:

> The two, lyrics and music, have always been dependent, in much the same way as a mannequin and a set of clothes are dependent on each other. Separate them, and what remains is a naked dummy and a pile of cloth.

So, I undressed my lyrics—but realized that the lyrics survived on their own, without the mannequin of visuals. If not all, a good majority of them survived in another genre or form—as poetry.

When Sunjoy translated a few of my lyrics into English, they sounded suspiciously like poems. I agreed to compile a hundred in book form, and was lucky to have a critical editor in Udayan Mitra who did not allow the translation to move away from the original context. My thanks to Pavan Jha for ensuring that we have the correct Hindi text for every lyric.

In a poem and a lyric, the major difference is that a poem is a personal expression of the poet, whereas in a lyric, the expression is primarily that of the character arising out of the situation of the film story. A poem is not necessarily singable, whereas a lyric has to be set to music—often adjusting the meter of the verse for the musical composition. In a literary poem, that would be ungrammatical.

While selecting the lyrics, we made sure that most of the themes were of a general nature, and included some popular lyrics, so that readers could easily identify with the situation.

I shall wait for your reactions, when you have read them!

Mumbai
20 June 2009

Translator's Preface

I grew up wearing the sound of Gulzarsaab's lyrics in my ears. Shards of his songs still reverberate in my ears from numerous occasions: '*Dakiya dak laya*' from a dark, rainy dawn in August twenty-eight years ago, playing on the Philips sound box; '*Mera kuchh samaan*' from a misty, foggy Delhi University December; '*Ek akela is shahar mein*' from an insipid hot unemployed afternoon in Mumbai. His songs have always evoked feelings, associations. And I am but a smuggler trying to surreptitiously smuggle the feelings those associations evoke in their original language across an impermissible alien wordscape.

Gulzar's lyrics transcend social barriers. A rickshawallah in the bylanes of Mumbai hums the tune of '*Chhaiyya chhaiyya*' without being aware of its literary merit, while an elite Urduwallah admires its tribute to Sufi traditions, wrapping it around himself over single malt on a cold cloudy Delhi evening. There is nothing in common between the two, but Gulzar touches them both. The rickshawallah banging his overused T-series tape recorder with his foot when the song stops in between is inarticulate, illiterate. But he too is stirred by Gulzar's evocation, he too lapses into euphoria like the Dilliwallah over his Scotch. A common thought shared in a familiar language weaves magic. Gulzar's lyrics are not just words, not just rhythm. They are a way of seeing and interpreting the world—the joy of being in it, the pain of it not being moulded after the heart's desires. In his lyrics Gulzar captures the very essence of India—its colours and its aroma—and makes it uniquely his. And I admit that such patterns can never be the same after the act of translation.

The Italians believe that a translator is essentially a traitor. They even have a phrase for it: *traduttore-traditore*. And I must confess that I do feel this. You work with a necessary handicap when you translate Gulzar's lyrics: the songs are so well known—the rendition, the music, the picturization—that they are permanently etched in the collective consciousness of the listeners. And to add to that, Gulzar's songs can still stand on their own, even if you were to strip them off the context of the film. Let us take the songs of *Lekin*. Everybody knows that the film is built around Dimple Kapadia's ghost—on the face of it the songs talk about life from the point of view of the ghost—but even if you take the movie out of the picture, it holds. Listening to Gulzar's songs are like unravelling layers and layers of meaning. And yet you need to keep the whole thing in context, you cannot take it too far away from the images already ingrained in the listeners' mind.

I try to liken my job to that of a jeweller who is asked not to fashion a new line of jewellery but has been given a collection of beautiful, sparkling gems, well cut, well chiselled—all he has to do is fit them in a frame, and he has to do it so carefully that the beauty of the gems comes out, so that each of their individual facets reflects light from all angles. I have tried to do the same. Whether I have succeeded is for you to judge.

Jakarta   Sunjoy Shekhar
1 July 2009

Translator's Acknowledgements

It took me about a year to work out these translations. This book is for you Geeta: for all those early mornings, before the break of dawn, when you looked for me on the pillow next to you and found me missing, found me at my keyboard instead trying to ferry Gulzar's thoughts from one language to another. You were the touchstone on which I tested my translations. Thank you for ruthlessly throwing away the ones that did not agree to your ears. Thank you for fighting with me over the turns and twists of every single phrase.

Thank you Gulzarsaab for never giving up on truant me, for your encouragement and kindness.

Thank you Udayan for your enthusiasm and for the most unusual compliment, 'Arrey yeh wala to main touch hi nahi kar paya.'

Thank you Babu Kedarnath Prasad for buying me that Philips mono soundbox way back in 1975 and that record of Gulzarsaab's songs.

Thank you Manoj Punjabi for temporarily taking the load off my schedule, or else this book would never have been complete.

Thank you Babu Subrat Sinha for letting me hound you a hundred times, one song at a time. Thank you my friend for allowing me to run to you, any time of the day or night, with the fresh translation of every song. These translations read better for your suggestions. Thank you for your unflinching support and unfailing enthusiasm. Thank you Thakur Vikram Abhishek Nahar Mall. A few phrases in these translations are actually yours. Thank you for your friendship. Thank you Babu Sammeir Mody (I wonder if I got the spelling of your name right, but what the heck, I got the essence of your explanations right—one out of two isn't bad, eh!).

Thank you Sachin Khot for your long-distance wake-up calls, for being at my elbow always and keeping count! Thank you Amit Jain for simply being there! And a special thank you to Pavan Jha for ensuring that the lyrics in Hindi are error-free. And last but not the least, my two ardent listeners, Timmy Abraham and Saurabh Swamy—thank you!

Here's to the smile on my daughter Gauraa's face which widened once she could finally fathom those songs (in translation) that her mother, father and *masis* would hum all day.

Mora gora ang lai le

The birth pangs of the my first film song 'Mora gora ang lai le' started when Bimalda (Bimal Roy) and Sachinda (S.D. Burman) explained the 'song situation' to me. Kalyani (Nutan) secretly admires Vikas (Ashok Kumar), and one night after winding up the kitchen work, she comes out humming this song.

Bimalda put a stop to it right there: this 'character' cannot step outside the house, singing, he said.

Sachinda raised his eyebrows: If she doesn't go out then how is she is going to sing in front of the father?

Bimalda argued: If she can listen to her father's Vaishnav poetry, why can't she sing it?

'This isn't a poem Dada . . . this is a song.'

'Then write a poem. She will sing the poem.'

'The song will be stifled inside the house.'

'Then bring her out in the courtyard. But she will not step outside the house.'

'Fine, if she will not step out then I am not going to compose this song,' Sachinda warned.

That was how my first 'song situation' was explained to me.

मेरा गोरा अंग लई ले
मोहे श्याम रंग दई दे
छुप जाऊंगी रात ही में
मोहे पी का संग दई दे

इक लाज रोके पैयां
इक मोह खींचे बैयां
जाऊं किधर, न जानूं
हमका कोई बताई दे

बदरी हटा के चंदा
चुपके से झाँकि चंदा
तोहे राहू लागे बैरी
मुस्काए जी जलाई के

कुछ खो दिया है पाई के
कुछ पा लिया गँवाई के
कहाँ ले चला है मनवा
मोहे बावरी बनाई के

1 Bandini (1963)

take away this fair complexion of mine, o Lord
paint me in dark colours
make me one with the night
walk me into the company of my beloved

but modesty shackles my feet
while desire tugs at my arms
I am in a quandary, o Lord
would you please guide me?

the rogue of a moon
parts the clouds, peeps in
laughs at my discomfiture—
may you, o moon, be forever
bedeviled by an eclipse

I've lost a part of me
and found a part of myself
where does this heart plan to take me
having thus crazed me in love?

हवाओं पे लिख दो, हवाओं के नाम
हम अनजान परदेसियों का सलाम

यह किसके लिए है, बता, किसके नाम
ओ पंछी, यह तेरा, सुरीला सलाम

शाख़ पर जब धूप आई
हाथ छूने के लिए
छाँव छम् से नीचे कूदी
हँसके बोली, आइए

यहाँ सुबह से खेला करती है शाम
हवाओं पे लिख दो . . .

चुलबुला यह पानी अपनी
राह बहना भूलकर
लेटे–लेटे आईना
चमका रहा है फूल पर

ये भोले–से चेहरे हैं, मासूम नाम
हवाओं पे लिख दो हवाओं के नाम
हम अनजान परदेसियों का सलाम –

2 Do Dooni Char (1968)

write down on these winds
the salutations of us unknown strangers

tell us o bird, whom do you sing for
your mellifluous salutations
write down on these winds
the salutations of us unknown strangers

when the sun climbs onto the branch
to touch it with its warmth
the shade jumps off onto the ground
chuckles and says, come catch me

here, the dawn frolics with the dusk
the impish water of the stream
forgets its restless flow
to glint mirrors at the flowers

write down on these winds
these innocent names of seraphic faces
write down the salutations of us unknown strangers

आजकल पाँव ज़मीं पर नहीं पड़ते मेरे
बोलो, देखा है कभी तुमने मुझे उड़ते हुए

जब भी थामा है तेरा हाथ तो देखा है
लोग कहते हैं कि बस हाथ की रेखा है
हमने देखा है दो तक़दीरों को जुड़ते हुए
आजकल पाँव ज़मीं पर नहीं पड़ते मेरे

नींद-सी रहती है, हल्का-सा नशा रहता है
रात-दिन आँखों में इक चेहरा बसा रहता है
पर-लगी आँखों को देखा है कभी उड़ते हुए
आजकल पाँव ज़मीं पर नहीं पड़ते मेरे

जाने क्या होता है, हर बात पे कुछ होता है
दिन में कुछ होता है और रात में कुछ होता है
थाम लेना, जो कभी देखो हमें उड़ते हुए
आजकल पाँव ज़मीं पर नहीं पड़ते मेरे
बोलो, देखा है कभी तुमने मुझे उड़ते हुए

3 Ghar (1978)

these days I cannot keep my feet on the ground anymore
tell me—have you ever seen me fly?

whenever I hold your hands in mine
I see the lines of your fate entwine with mine
I just cannot keep my feet on the ground
no, no more
tell me—have you ever seen me fly?

these days a languor lives in my gait, a stupor in my eyes
only one image dwells in the eyes throughout the day
and throughout the night
have you ever seen the eyes put on their wings and fly?

something's afoot these days, every little thing sets me
    aflutter
something different in the day and something different
    at night
hold me to you if you ever see me flying
these days I just cannot keep my feet on the ground
tell me—have you ever seen me fly?

आने वाला पल, जाने वाला है
हो सके तो इस में
ज़िंदगी बिता दो
पल जो ये जाने वाला

इक बार यूँ मिली
मासूम सी कली
खिलते हुए कहा
ख़ुशबाश मैं चली

देखा तो यहीं है
ढूँढा तो नहीं है
पल जो ये जाने वाला है
आने वाला पल . . .

इक बार वक़्त से
लम्हा गिरा कहीं
वहाँ दास्ताँ मिली
लम्हा कहीं नहीं
थोड़ा सा हँसाके
थोड़ा सा रुलाके

पल ये भी जाने वाला है
आने वाला पल . . .

4 Gol Maal (1979)

this moment that is
about to come
is about to flit away
live your life if you can
in this fleeting moment

once I saw an innocent bud
and it said to me—
between my blossoming and my wilting
I live a fleeting life, but look
how fragrant I make this life to be

I just saw this moment here, upon us
but the moment I look for it
that moment is gone

once a moment
fell off from time
but the moment it fell it was gone
leaving only a tale to tell in its wake

a little laughter, a few drops of tears
is the only promise that it holds—
this moment that is about to come
and about to flit away

रात का . . . शौक़ है
रात की . . .
सौंधी ख़ामोशी का, शौक़ है
शौक़ है . . .

सुबह की . . . रौशनी
बेजुबां सुबह की
गुनगुनाती रौशनी का, शौक़ है
शौक़ है . . .

रात की, ख़ामोशी . . . बेजुबां सुबह का, शौक़ है

नीन्द की . . . गोलियों का
ख़्वाब की . . . लोरियों का

नीन्द की . . . गोलियाँ
ख़्वाब की . . . लोरियाँ
बेजुबां, ओस की, बोलियों का, शौक़ है

काश ये ज़िन्दगी ख़्वाब ही, ख़्वाब की, ज़िन्दगी होती

सन्सनी, नावलों का
इशक़ के, बावलों का
बर्फ़ से खेलते बादलों का . . . शौक़ है

काश ये, ज़िन्दगी, खेल ही खेल में, खो गई होती!

5 Guru (2007)

I have a predilection
for the night
for the aromatic silence of the night

I have a predilection
for the brightness of the morning
for the trilling brightness of the voiceless morning

I have a predilection
for pills to ease my troubled sleep
for lullabies to string my dreams
for the prattle of voiceless dewdrops

wish this life could go to sleep
without hearing a word
without uttering a word

I have a predilection
for racy thrilling novels
for love-crazed lunatics
for snowflakes dancing down the clouds

wish this life could be gambolled away
in a child's innocent play

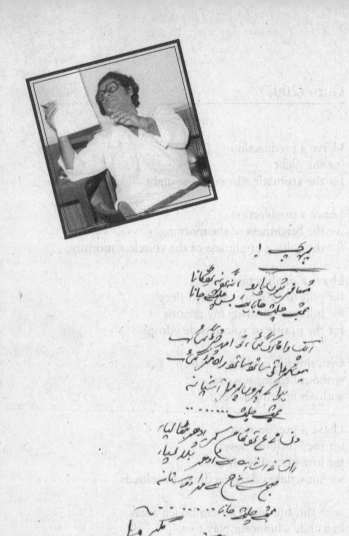

پیارے چینی !

مسافر ہوں یارو ، نہ گھر ہے نہ ٹھکانا
محبت بھری چھاؤں ، بس چلتے جانا

آگے واقفِ زبانی نہ امیدوں کا سہارا
پیچھے خالی کاسہ ، قافلہ نظر نہیں

پیار کے بول پیار ملا ، اشیانہ
بس چلے ....

دن تم نے قوم نام کر دھوکا لیا
رات بھر نہ سو ، سحر بند کیا
صبح سے شام ، ہم زندگانی
محبت بھری چھاؤں ، بس چلتے جانا

पंचम के साथ ये पहला गाना था मेरा—

राज कमल स्टूडियो में किसी पिक्चर का बैक-ग्राउंड म्यूज़िक चल रहा था। स्टूडियो जाते हुए उसने मुझे घर से साथ ले लिया। सिचुएशन मैं उसे पहले बता चुका था। गाड़ी में जाते जाते उसने कहा—'मुझे अभी तक कुछ सूझा नहीं! कोई मुखड़ा दे, मैं उस पर धुन बना लूंगा।' दो चार उड़ते मुड़ते ख़्याल आये। स्टूडियो पहुंचने पर मैंने ये लाइनें उसे लिखवा दीं।

मुसाफ़िर हूं यारो, न घर न ठिकाना
मुझे बस चलते जाना है बस चलते जाना

लाइनें नोट कर के उसने मेरा पैकअप कर दिया—'तू जा। मुझे बहुत काम है।' ये उसका हमेशा का रवैया था—

उसी रात क़रीब बारह बजे मेरे घर पे दस्तक हुई—और उसने मुझे जगा के पूछा: 'क्या सो रहा था? चल नीचे गाड़ी में!' नीचे गाड़ी में, उसने कैसेट लगाया और धुन सुनाई। वाकई कमाल की तर्ज़ थी। बम्बई की ख़ाली सड़कों पर वो गाड़ी चलाता रहा और मुखड़ा गाता रहा। धीरे धीरे धुन आगे बढ़ने लगी। मैं आगे की लाइनें बनाता गया और वो गाता रहा। बम्बई में, रात की सड़कों पर मुसाफ़िरों की तरह घूमते घूमते, सुबह चार बजे तक हमने गाना पूरा कर लिया . . .!

इसी गाने से हमारा सांझा सफ़र जारी हुआ!

13

मुसाफ़िर हूँ यारो . . . न घर है, न ठिकाना
मुझे चलते जाना है, बस चलते जाना

एक राह रुक गई, तो और जुड़ गई
मैं मुड़ा तो साथ साथ, राह मुड़ गई

हवा के परों पर . . . मेरा आशियाना . . .
मुसाफ़िर हूँ यारो . . .

दिन ने हाथ थामकर, इधर बिठा लिया
रात ने इशारे से, उधर बुला लिया

सुबह से शाम से, मेरा दोस्ताना
मुसाफ़िर हूँ यारो . . .

6 Parichay (1972)

I am but a wanderer, my friends
no home, no address
wandering is all I am here to do

where one road stops
another joins
when I turn
the road too
curves along with me

I nestle
on the wings of the wind
I am but a wanderer

the day takes my hand
brings me here
the night beckons me
and calls me there

the dusk and the dawn
I have as my friends
I am but a wanderer

मैं एक सदी से बैठी हूं
इस राह से कोई गुजरा नहीं
कुछ चाँद के रथ तो गुज़रे थे
पर चाँद से कोई उतरा नहीं

दिन रात के दोनों पहिए भी
कुछ धूल उड़ा कर बीत गए
मैं मन आंगन में बैठी रही
चौखट से कोई गुज़रा नहीं
मैं एक सदी से बैठी हूँ . . .

आकाश बड़ा बूढ़ा बाबा
सब को कुछ बाँट के जाता है
आँखों को निचोड़ा मैंने बहुत
पर कोई आँसू उतरा नहीं
मैं एक सदी से बैठी हूँ . . .

7 Lekin (1991)

I have been waiting
a hundred years
nobody's passed by this path
a few moons
did chariot through
but not a soul disembarked

I have been waiting
by the threshold of my heart
the twin wheels of day and night too
left just bursts of dirt in their wake
but not a soul breezed across

the old man sky
bequeaths something
to everyone
all I ask is a few drops—
but however hard I wring my eyes
not a single teardrop falls

जनम से बंजारा हूँ बंधू, जनम जनम बंजारा
कहीं कोई घर न घाट न अंगनारा

जहाँ कहीं ठहर गया दिल, हमने डाले डेरे
रात कहीं नमकीन मिली तो मीठे सांझ सवेरे
कभी नगरी छोड़ी, साहिल छोड़ा, लिया मंझधारा
जनम से बंजारा . . .

सोच ने जब करवट बदली, शौक़ ने पर फैलाए
मैंने आशियाँ के तिनके सारे डाल से उड़ाए
कभी रिश्ते तोड़े, नाते तोड़े, छोड़ा कूल किनारा
जनम से बंजारा . . .

8 Raahgir (1969)

I am a nomad by birth, my friend—
a nomad in every birth, every reincarnation—
not fettered to any house, not bound to any shore

I followed the heart
camped at its diktat
embraced sultry salty nights
and sweet dawns and dusks

at times I fled the cities
at others I forsook
the calm of the shores
to join the river flow
I am a nomad by birth, my friend

at the turn of thoughts
I have spread my wings
and flapped away
the twigs of my nest—
forfeiting relationships
snapping all ties—
and I have flown to follow my heart

I am a nomad by birth my friend
a nomad in every birth, every reincarnation

जीवन से लम्बे हैं बन्धू, ये जीवन के रस्ते
इक पल थम के रोना होगा, इक पल चलना हँसके

राहों से राही का रिश्ता कितने जनम पुराना
एक को चलते जाना आगे, एक को पीछे आना

मोड़ पे मत रुक जाना बन्धू, दोराहों में फँस के
जीवन से लम्बे हैं बन्धू . . .

दिन और रात के हाथों नापी, नापी एक उमरिया
सांस की डोरी छोटी पड़ गई लम्बी आस डगरिया

भोर के मन्जिल वाले, उठ कर भोर से पहले चलते
ये जीवन के रास्ते . . .
जीवन से लम्बे हैं बन्धू . . .

9 Aashirwad (1968)

the paths of life
are lengthier than life itself, o friend—
a moment to stop and cry
a moment to laugh and be onward bound again

eternal are the ties that bind the traveller to the road
one leads, the other follows

and when you come to a crossroads, o friend
beware—
do not stop, move on
for the paths
of life are lengthier than life itself

even if you have measured a lifetime
by the span of days and nights
you will still find the thread of breath
too short and the strides of hope too long

so, remember o friend
that those whose destination is the dawn
embark on their journey before the day breaks in

the paths of life o friend
are lengthier than life itself

एक अकेला इस शहर में
रात में और दोपहर में
आब–ओ–दाना ढूँढता है
आशियाना ढूँढता है

दिन ख़ाली ख़ाली बर्तन है
और रात है जैसे अंधा कुआँ
इन सूनी अंधेरी आँखों में
आँसू की जगह आता है धुँआं

जीने की वजह तो कोई नहीं
मरने का बहाना ढूँढता है . . .
एक अकेला . . .

इन उम्र से लम्बी सड़कों को
मंज़िल पे पहुँचते देखा नहीं
बस दौड़ती फिरती रहती हैं
हम ने तो ठहरते देखा नहीं

इस अजनबी से शहर में
जाना पहचाना ढूँढता है . . .
एक अकेला . . .

10 Gharonda (1977)

all alone in this city
he wanders from dawn to dusk
in search of a livelihood
in quest for a shelter, a roof

the days are empty pots and pans
the nights are bottomless wells
no tears—just smoke
billows from
his dark dejected eyes

no reason to live
all he searches for
is an excuse to die

relentlessly on the run
these roads
longer than a lifetime
lead him
nowhere

from dusk to dawn
all alone
he still searches for a familiar face
in this sea of unfamiliarity

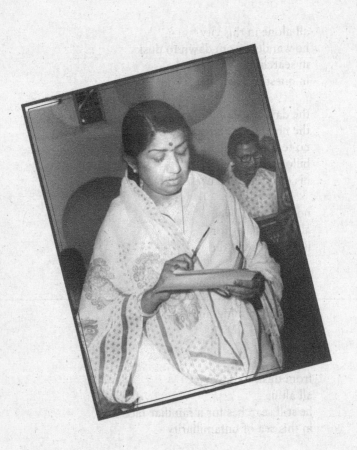

Humne dekhi hai un ankhon ki mehekti khushboo . . .

One of the earliest songs of mine, where I used very abstract images, like 'aroma of those eloquent eyes'. I was heavily criticized and even teased for writing this kind of poetry. But thanks to Hemant Kumar (the composer and the producer), who was a celebrated singer of Tagore's songs and could easily relate to this kind of imagery, the song worked. But its gender changed. The song was a male adoration of the beloved's eyes, but was sung by a female singer. Only Lataji could change the gender of a song!

ख़ामोशी (१९७०)

हमने देखी है उन आँखों की महकती ख़ुशबू
हाथ से छू के इसे रिश्तों का इलज़ाम न दो
सिर्फ़ एहसास है यह, रूह से महसूस करो
प्यार को प्यार ही रहने दो, कोई नाम न दो

प्यार कोई बोल नहीं, प्यार आवाज़ नहीं
एक ख़ामोशी है, सुनती है, कहा करती है
न यह बुझती है, न रुकती है, न ठहरी है कहीं
नूर की बूँद है, सदियों से बहा करती है

हमने देखी है उन आँखों की महकती ख़ुशबू...

मुस्काहट-सी खिली रहती है आंखों में कहीं
और पलकों पे उजाले से झुके रहते हैं
होंठ कुछ कहते नहीं, कांपते होंठों पे मगर
कितने ख़ामोश से अफ़साने रुके रहते हैं

हमने देखी है उन आँखों की महकती ख़ुशबू...

11 Khamoshi (1970)

I have seen the wafting aroma of those eloquent eyes
do not touch it with your hands and stamp it with a
    relationship
it's just a sensation, caress it with your soul
let love be love, do not label it

love is not in words, love is not in sounds
love is just a silence that speaks, that hears
love is unstoppable, love is inextinguishable
love is a droplet of light shimmering through the ages

something like a smile is in bloom somewhere in those eyes
something like sunshine lingers around those eyelids
the lips don't say a word, but numerous unspoken stories
hover around their quivering edges

I have seen the wafting aroma of those eloquent eyes

आस्माँ के पार, शायद, और कोई आस्मां होगा
बादलों के पर्वत पर, कोई बारिश का मकाँ होगा
मैं हवा के परों पे कहाँ, जा रहा हूं कहाँ
कभी उड़ता हुआ, कभी मुड़ता हुआ, मेरा रास्ता चला

इन लम्बे रास्तों पर सब तेज़ चलते होंगे
कापी के पन्नों जैसे यहां दिन पलटते होंगे

शाम को भी, सुबह जैसा, क्या समाँ होगा
आस्मां के पार, शायद . . .

मेरे पाँव के तले की ये ज़मीन चल रही है
कहीं धूप ठंडी ठंडी कहीं छाँव जल रही है

इस ज़मीं का, और कोई, आस्मां होगा
आस्मां के, पार शायद

beyond this sky, there must be yet another sky
on the mountains of the clouds, there must be the
    abode of rain
on the wings of the breeze, I am off somewhere, where
my path twirls, at times soaring, at times forking

on these long roads, everybody must be rushing along
like the leaves of notebooks, the days must be turning
    too

the evenings, like mornings, must be dazzling bright
beyond this sky, there must be yet another sky

the ground beneath my feet is moving
the sunshine's nippy, the shade's burning bright

for this earth, there must be another sky
beyond this sky, there must be yet another sky

आ धूप मलूं मैं तेरे हाथों में
आ सजदा करूं मैं तेरे हाथों में
सुबह की मेहंदी छलक रही है
आ जा, आ जा माहिया

आहिस्ता पुकारो, सब सुन लेंगे
बस लबों से छू लो, लब सुन लेंगे
आ सांस भी कब से अटक रही है
आ जा माहिया . . .

इक नूर से आंखें चौंक गईं
देखा जो तुझे आईने में
कोई नूरी किरन होगी वो भी
जो चुभने लगी है सीने में
आ जा माहिया . . .

लाल हो जब ये शाम किनारा
ओढ़ा देना सर पे सारा
आ जा माहिया . . .

चल रोक लें सूरज, छुप जाएगा
पानी में गिर के, बुझ जाएगा
आ जा माहिया . . .

13 Fiza (2000)

come, o beloved
let me rub sunlight into your palms
let me place my forehead in your palms and pray
let's see the hennaed rays spill off your palms

hush! don't make a sound
they are all ears
see, the lips quiver
silence them with the seal of your lips
hurry—
I am barely able to hold on to my breath

when I see you in the mirror
the light reflected off your image
dazzles the eye
it must be that dazzling ray
that sears my heart

and when the shore's a molten red
pluck the evening and wrap it over my head

come, o beloved
let's stop the sun before it slinks away
before it falls into the river and drowns

ओ साथी रे, दिन डूबे ना
आ चल दिन को रोकें
धूप के पीछे दौड़ें
छांव छुए ना . . . ओ पीहू रे

थका थका सूरज जब
नदी से होकर निकलेगा
हरी हरी काई पर
पांव पड़ा तो फिसलेगा

तुम रोक के रखना
मैं जाल गिराऊं
तुम पीठ पे लेना
मैं हाथ लगाऊं
    ओ साथी रे . . . दिन डूबे ना . . .

तेरी मेरी अट्टी–बट्टी
दांत से काटी कट्टी
    रे जाइयो ना . . . ओ पीहू रे

कभी कभी, यूं करना
मैं डांटू और तुम डरना
उबल पड़े आंखों से
मीठे पानी का झरना

14 Omkara (2006)

my love, my beloved—
wish the day never ends
come, let's arrest the day
let's run for the sun
lest the shadows grip us

when the overworked, droopy
sun steps on to the river
from the mossy banks
he is wont to slip—
let's grab him then
you tarry him a little
I'll drop the mesh
you haul him on your back
I will give you a hand—
wish the day never ends

if you go away, my love
I will never speak with you—
I swear

and sometimes, let's play pretend
I will scold you and you be scared
and let a fountain of fresh water
spring from your eyes

तेरे दोहरे बदन में
सिल जाऊँगी रे
जब करवट ले आ
छिल जाऊँगी रे
    ओ साथी रे . . . ओ पीहू रे

संग ले जाऊँगा
तेरी मेरी अंगनी मंगनी
अंग संग लागी संगनी
संग ले जाऊँ

I will stitch myself onto your body
so inseparable that
I'll bruise even if
you turn on your side

o my love, my beloved
wish the day never ends

मैंने तेरे लिए ही सात रंग के सपने चुने
सपने, सुरीले सपने
हँसते, कुछ ग़म के, तेरी आंखों के साए
चुराए, रसीली यादों ने

छोटी बातें, छोटी छोटी बातों की हैं यादें बड़ी
भूले नहीं, बीती हुई एक छोटी घड़ी
जनम जनम से आंखे बिछाई तेरे लिए इन राहों ने
मैंने तेरे लिए ही . . .

भोले भाले, दिल को बहलाते रहे
तन्हाई में, तेरे ख़्यालों को सजाते रहे
कभी कभी तो आवाज़ देकर, मुझको जगाया ख़्वाबों ने
मैंने तेरे लिए ही . . .

रूठी रातें, रूठी हुई रातों को जगाया कभी
तेरे लिए बीती सुबह को बुलाया कभी
तेरे बिना भी तेरे लिए ही, दिये जलाये राहों में
मैंने तेरे लिए ही . . .

15 Anand (1971)

I culled all the seven colours
in the weave of your dreams
and arranged them
on the seven notes of melody

a few notes of laughter
a few notes of grief—
cast-off shadows of your eyes
I have stolen to flavour my memories

it is the little things that carve
a big chunk of memory
I haven't forgotten even
a fraction of a moment spent with you
I have been born again and again
only to be with you

I have always populated
my loneliness with your thoughts
amused my innocent heart—
and at times, when I fell asleep
dreams of you called out to me
and woke me up

and when the nights were estranged
I placated them for you
and ushered in dulcet mornings—
even without you, I kept lighting lamps
along the passage you would come by

بیٹیاں

پہلے سے دنیا میں بیٹیاں کم
حجرہ بعد میں بھی خالی ہے بیٹیاں کم

یہاں کو ساہل بہلا نہیں ہے
کہیں کوئی ڈھب کو کنارا نہیں ہے
یہاں سارے ورق پہ رسوائیاں کم
تم جو اندر کہ کر چلائے بجبائے
بہت ہم نے چاہ کر ارینہ گئے
یہاں راس بیٹیوں سے بہاریاں کم
یہاں سے ....

یہاں سارے چہرے پر مانگے نورس
کئی سال میں دھوبی بھی ٹانگ نورس
پھر نیچے داس سب لوٹجایئاں کم
یہاں سے ....

ये गाना एक फ़िल्म ऐक्ट्रैस का गाना है। फ़िल्म में वो ऐक्ट्रैस है—और दिन रात की रोशनियों तले थक गई है। सब कुछ मांगा मांगा, उधार लिया हुआ लगता है। यहां तक ज़िंदगी भी उधार की लगने लगी है। ये लिखते हुये मीना जी बहुत याद आई। वो अक्सर एक शेर सुनाया करती थीं।

एक धड़का सा लगा रहता है खो जाने का
जीस्त हमसाये से मांगा हुआ ज़ेवर तो नहीं

शायर का नाम न उन्होंने बताया। न मुझे मिला . . . !

ये साए हैं, नये ये दुनिया है परछाइयों की
भरी भीड़ में, ख़ाली तन्हाइयों की

यहां कोई साहिल-सहारा नहीं है
कहीं डूबने को किनारा नहीं है

यहां सारी रौनक है रूसवाइयों की
यह साए हैं, ये दुनिया है परछाइयों की

कई चांद उठकर जलाए-बुझाए
बहुत हमने चाहा ज़रा नींद आए

यहां रात होती है बेदारियों की
यह साए हैं, दुनिया है परछाइयों की . . .

यहां सारे चेहरे हैं मांगे हुए-से
निगाहों में आंसू भी टांगे हुए-से

बड़ी नीची राहें हैं ऊंचाइयों की
यह साए हैं, दुनिया है परछाइयों की . . .
भरी भीड़ में, ख़ाली तन्हाइयों की . . .

16 Sitara (1980)

it's a spectre, this world
of shadows—
a throng of cavernous loneliness

no support here, not even a shore in sight
to drown yourself at

all the elegance here is of disgrace
the splendour here is of dishonour

it's a spectre, this world
of shadows—

many a moon have I lit and snuffed out
but couldn't snatch even a few winks of sleep
the night only brings wakefulness
it's a spectre, this world
of shadows—

here, the teardrops are stitched
on faces that are borrowed
here, in this world of spectres
the path to the zenith
runs through the nadir

दिल के सन्नाटे खोल कभी
तन्हाई तू भी बोल कभी

परछाइयां चुनता रहता है
क्यों रिश्ते बुनता रहता है
इन वादों के पीछे कोई नहीं
क्यों वादे सुनता रहता है

बुझ जाएंगी सारी आवाज़ें
यादें यादें रह जाएंगी
तस्वीरें बचेंगी आंखों में
और बातें सब बह जाएंगी

दिल के सन्नाटे खोल कभी
तन्हाई तू भी बोल कभी . . .

17 Filhaal (2002)

shatter the silences of the heart
loneliness—find a voice

must you
glean shadows
forge relationships
listen to promises
bereft of honour

the voices will be doused
the memories will turn stale
the promises will drain away
and all that will remain
are the debris of images
drifting in the eyes

shatter the silences of the heart

जाने कैसे बीतेंगी ये बरसातें
मांगे हुए हैं दिन, मांगी हुई रातें

धुआं धुआं सा रहता है
बुझी बुझी सी आंखों में
सुलग रहे हैं गीले आँसू
आग लगाती हैं ये बरसातें
        जाने कैसे बीतेंगी . . .

भरा हुआ था दिल शायद
छलक गया है सीने में
बहने लगे हैं सारे शिकवे
बड़ी ग़मगीं हैं दिल की बातें
        जाने कैसे बीतेंगी . . .

18 Baseraa (1981)

how am I supposed to
tide through these downpours—
the days are pawned
and the nights taken out on loan

smoke drifts in these eyes
from embers of extinguished hopes
and the damp tears
set ablaze by the rain

the heart was full to the brim, perhaps
it spills its complaints over onto the chest
plaintive are
the tales of the heart

दिन जा रहे हैं रातों के साए
अपनी सलीबें आप ही उठाए

जब कोई डूबा रातों का तारा
कोई सवेरा वापस न आया

वापस जो आए, वीरान साए
दिन जा रहे हैं रातों के साए . . .

जीना तो कोई मुश्किल नहीं था
मगर डूबने को साहिल नहीं था

साहिल से कोई अब तो बुलाए
दिन जा रहे हैं रातों के साए . . .

सांसों की डोरी टूटे न टूटे
ज़रा ज़िंदगी से दामन तो छूटे

कोई ज़िंदगी के हाथ न आए
दिन जा रहे हैं रातों के साए . . .

the days trudge
like spectres of the night
carrying their own crosses

there's no morning to the night
whose bright star drowns—
no second coming

all that ever come back are
sepulchral shadows, carrying
their crosses—trudging along

I forced myself
to go on living
for I found no river to plunge in
wish somebody would
call me back to life

I am tied to the apron strings of life
tied by these strings of breath, strings
that do not snap however hard I try

I wish
nobody gets caught
in the claws of life

मेरे साथ चले न साया . . .
धर्म नहीं, कर्म नहीं . . . जन्म गंवाया

मेरे लिए दिन भी अन्धेरा
मेरे लिए रात भी लाए न सवेरा

जो दे उजाला, दे सवेरा
वही मेरा हमसाया
धर्म नहीं, कर्म नहीं . . . जन्म गंवाया

मेरे लिए, जगत भी सौतेला
भरी हुई भीड़ में रहा अकेला

जो दे सहारा, दे किनारा
वही मेरा हमसाया
धर्म नहीं, कर्म नहीं . . . जन्म गंवाया

20 Kitaab (1977)

my shadow does not walk
with me anymore
I have wasted this birth of mine
without any faith, any deeds

for me the day is
an unbroken expanse of darkness
and the night
does not bring in its wake
a morning
and I am looking for a friend
someone who will brighten my darkness
someone who will usher in the morning

this world has treated me like a stepson
and I find myself alone in its teeming billions

forsaken by my own shadow
adrift in this void, without any beliefs
I am looking for a friend
to guide me ashore, to give me faith—
to rescue me from myself

لباس

پہلی نوا چھیڑی اسی پیار میں چلی گئی
پہلی نظر سے جڑے سیلاب آنند نکل گیا

جانے کہاں کہیے گر
لکھے جملے پہ دل معطب

ترے گیسوؤں دل نہ جلا
ترے لبوں غضب نہ بجھے

جتنے کہوں طے کے رنگ
لبوں گشت پہ خاکہ لے

میلوں مدن چھوڑ دیتے
سالوں سی راہ اے کر چلے
پہلی نوا چھوڑ گیا ....

غالب اللہ

'लिबास' एक अलग की तरह की पोशाक़ थी, थिएटर बैक-ग्राउंड पर एक कहानी थी। 'चाबी' के नाम से मेरे पहले मजमुए में छपी थी। थिएटर के कैरेक्टर्स में एक अजीब तरह की फुरती होती है। उसके मूड भी लिबास की तरह बदलते रहते है। लिबास ही की तरह दिन पहनते हैं और उतार देते हैं। कुछ ऐसी ही कैफ़ियत इस गाने में है। मुझे अफ़सोस है कि ये फ़िल्म कभी रीलीज़ न हो सकी।

सीली हवा छू गई
सीला बदन छिल गया
नीली नदी के परे
गीला सा चांद खिल गया

जाने कहां कैसे शहर
ले के चला ये दिल मुझे
तेरे बग़ैर दिन ना जला
तेरे बग़ैर शब ना बुझे

जितने भी तय करते गए
बढ़ते गए ये फ़ासले
मीलों से दिन छोड़ आए
सालों सी रात ले के चले

तुम से मिली जो ज़िन्दगी
हम ने अभी बोई नहीं
तेरे सिवा कोई न था
तेरे सिवा कोई नहीं

सीली हवा छू गई . . .

the dank air touches me
scrapes my clammy body
a wet moon blossoms
across the blue river

without you—
I am but a rudderless traveller
unanchored in the night
and the night refuses to die out
the dawn refuses to break in

the gulf—
separating us
yawns further
I swap my mile-long day
with the night
and the night
stretches itself into years

the life—
you had gifted me
it hasn't blossomed
I haven't sown it yet, for
what use would it be without you

without you, beyond you
there's nothing but a dank, dark hollowness

छोड़ आए हम वो गलियां . . .
जहां तेरे पैरों के कंवल गिरा करते थे
हंसे तो दो गालों में, भंवर पड़ा करते थे
तेरी कमर के बल पे नदी मुड़ा करती थी
हंसी तेरी सुन सुनके फ़सल पका करती थी
　　छोड़ आये हम वो गलियां . . .

जहां तेरी एढी से धूप उड़ा करती थी
सुना है उस चौखट पे, अब शाम रहा करती है
लटों से उलझी लिपटी इक रात हुआ करती थी
कभी कभी तकिये पे वो भी मिला करती है
　　छोड़ आये हम वो गलियां . . .

दिल दर्द का टुकड़ा है, पत्थर की डली सी है
इक अंधा कुंआं है, या इक बंद गली सी है
इक छोटा सा लम्हा है, जो ख़त्म नही होता
मैं लाख जलाता हूं, ये भस्म नहीं होता
　　छोड़ आये हम वो गलियां . . .

22 Maachis (1996)

we have abandoned those lanes
where lotuses blossomed on footfalls of yours
where laughter whirlpooled on your dimpled cheeks
where the rivers pirouetted at the twirl of your waist
where the crops ripened with the sprinkle of your
    laughter
we have abandoned those lanes

where sunshine fluttered around your ankles
on those doorways, I have heard
only dusk hangs these days
a night would take refuge in your dark tresses
sometimes, I meet those nights
on my pillow

the heart's a sliver of pain
just a chunk of stone
an abyss, a bottomless pit, or just a blind alley
a mere fragmented moment that's never over
often I have tried to burn it
but it does not turn to ashes

वो शाम कुछ अजीब थी
ये शाम भी अजीब है
वो कल भी पास पास थी
वो आज भी क़रीब है

झुकी हुई निगाह में
कहीं मेरा ख़्याल था
दबी दबी हंसी में इक
हसीन सा गुलाल था

मैं सोचता था मेरा नाम
गुनगुना रही है वो
न जाने क्यों लगा मुझे
कि मुस्करा रही है वो

मेरा ख़्याल है अभी
झुकी हुई निगाह में
खिली हुई हंसी भी है
दबी हुई सी चाह में

मैं जानता हूं मेरा नाम
गुनगुना रही है वो
यही ख़्याल है मुझे
कि साथ आ रही है वो

that evening was a little enigmatic
enigmatic, this evening too
she was close by me even then
she's nearby even now

somewhere in those lowered eyes
nestled a thought of me
something in that hushed laughter
brought a glow to her rosy cheeks

and it seemed
as if my name was lingering on her lips
don't know why it felt
as if she was beaming a smile at me

I think thoughts of me
are still ensconced in that
lowered gaze of hers
a smile must still bloom
in that stifled desire

I know that my name
still lingers on her lips
and I think
she's still here with me

that evening was a little enigmatic
enigmatic, this evening too

बंजर है सब बंजर है
हम ढूंढने जब फ़िरदौस चले
तेरी खोज तलाश में देखा पिया
हम कितने काले कोस चले
बंजर है सब बंजर है

मेंडा यार मिला दे साइयां
एक बार मिला दे साइयां

मैंने पोटा पोटा फ़लक छाना
मैंने टोटे टोटे तारे चुने
सिर्फ़ एक तेरी आहट के लिए
कंकड़ पत्थर बुत सारे सुने
उड़ें वेने ते रूसवाइयाँ

तारों की चमक ये सुबह तलक
लगती ही नहीं पल भर को पलक
साइयां साइयां . . .

आ देख मेरी पेशानी को, तक़दीर के हर्फ़ें लिखें हैं
मैं कितनी बार पुकारूं तुझे तेरे नाम के सफ़े लिखें हैं
तेरा साया कभी तो बोलेगा
मैं चुनता रहा हूं परछाइयां
मेंडा यार मिला दे साइयां
साइयां साइयां . . .

beloved, in your search
I have rummaged through
a million dark miles
but the pursuit of paradise yields—
only wilderness

unite me with my beloved, o lord
just one more time, o lord

beloved, in your search
I have frisked every patch of sky
but all I felt in my grasp
were shards of broken stars

for just one sound of yours
I listened to every pebble, stone and icon
but all that I heard were taunts and sneers

the shimmering stars
abandoned the night sky
like sleep deserted my expectant eyes

come hither, have a look—
see the hieroglyphics of fate
chiselled on my forehead
all chanting your name
I have begun to trail all shadows
in the hope they may lead to you

unite me just one more time
with my beloved, o lord

यारा सीली सीली
बिरहा की आग में जलना

ये भी कोई जीना है
ये भी कोई मरना

टूटी हुई चूड़ियों से
जोड़ूं ये कलाई मैं
पिछली गली में जाने
क्या छोड़ आई मैं

बीती हुई गलियों से
फिर से गुज़रना . . . यारा सीली सीली . . .

पैरों में ना साया कोई
सर पे ना साईं रे
मेरे साथ जाए ना
मेरी परछाई रे

बाहर उजाड़ा है
अंदर वीराना . . . यारा सीली सीली . . .

25 Lekin (1991)

o beloved, I am burning
in this damp, dank fire
of separation

is this a life worth living
is this any way to die

o beloved, I am trying to
adorn my wrist with bits of broken bangles
carrying the pieces
from the alleys of my past
condemned to revisit
those lanes yet again

forsaken by you
deserted by my own shadow
I have to tread all over again
on splinters of my past
with nothing to cushion my bare feet
just a wilderness outside
and an emptiness within

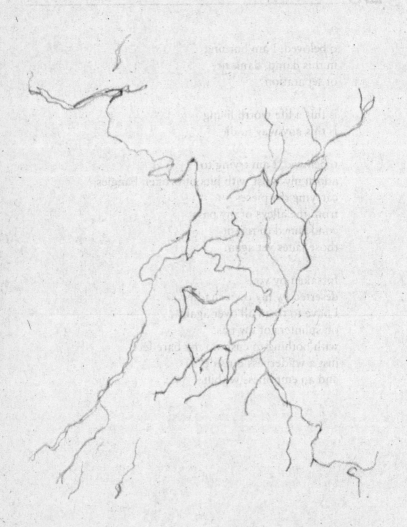

This was for a non-film album. I was travelling with two souls who were desperately in love. They met over a sunset, and that became their meeting point.

They wished to do something out of the world, and I was asked to provide the options.

one . . . two . . . let's jump off the moon

They meet again at the top of a rotating tower in Toronto:

आसमानी आंखों का आसमानी रंग है, आंखों में बहने दो . . .

The entire imagery is abstract and never lands on earth. For me it was like gaining freedom from a film situation, but not free from a storyline.

आ चल डूब के देखें
एक-दो, चाँद से कूदें

आँखों की कश्ती में
रात बिताई जाए
झीलों के पानी पे
नींद बिछाई जाए
चलो न डूबें . . .
आ चल डूब के देखें
एक-दो, चाँद से कूदें
आ . . .

चल दरिया बाँध लें पैरों से
और सागर संगम जाएँ
चल सनसेट के रंग पहनें तन पे
बुद्धम् शरणम् गाएं
कुछ ऐसा करें जो हुआ नहीं
जो हुआ नहीं वो करें
चलो न उड़ लें . . .

चल जेबें भर लें तारों से
दावें मिटकाते चलें
चल मफलर पहन के बादल के
बारिश बरसातें चलें
चलो ना डूबे . . .

come, let's drown ourselves
one . . . two . . . let's jump off the moon

let's sail the night in the boat of your eyes
let's still the waters of these lakes with sleep
come, let's drown ourselves

come, let's strap the river onto our feet
and rush down to the sea
come, let's wear the ochre of the sunset
and sing *Buddham sharanam*
come, let's do something that has not been done before
let's spread our wings and fly
let's fill our pockets with stars
and flit, sprinkling stardust

come, let's wear the muffler of the clouds
and fly, showering rain
come, let's drown ourselves—
in love

तुम आ गए हो नूर आ गया है
नहीं तो, चिरागों से लौ जा रही थी
जीने की तुमसे वजह मिल गई है
बड़ी बेवजह जिंदगी जा रही थी

कहां से चले, कहां के लिए, ये ख़बर नहीं थी मगर
कोई भी सिरा जहां जा मिला, वहीं तुम मिलोगे

कि हम तक तुम्हारी दुआ आ रही थी
तुम आ गए हो नूर आ गया है . . .

दिन डूबा नहीं, रात डूबी नहीं जाने कैसा है ये सफ़र
ख़्वाबों के दिये, आंखों में लिए, वहीं आ रहे थे

जहां से तुम्हारी सदा आ रही थी
तुम आ गए हो नूर आ गया है . . .

now that you have come, everything is illuminated
the flames would have died out from the lamps, otherwise

in you I have found a reason to live
life would've meandered into meaninglessness, otherwise

in your search I let myself drift rudderless, unaware
where the journey began, or where it was headed
rooted only in the belief that I would find you
wherever this road meets the other end, for—
your prayers were reaching out to me

what sort of a journey is this—
the day does not set, the night refuses to rest
and with hopes lit in my eyes I am headed off
to the place from where I heard
your voice calling out to me

and now
that you have come, everything is illuminated

देखो तो आसमान तारों से भर गया
दिल ये क्या कर गया . . .

नब्ज़ रुकने लगी, सांस बजने लगे
तिरछे तिरछे मेरे पांव पड़ने लगे
जाने क्यूं मैं डर गया
दिल ये क्या कर गया

किसने आवाज़ दी, कोई साया था क्या?
पीछे पीछे मेरे कोई आया था क्या?
डूब के मैं तर गया
दिल ये क्या कर गया . . .

देखो तो आसमान तारों से भर गया
दिल ये क्या कर गया . . .

what is this that my heart has wrought—
look, the sky's suddenly teeming with stars

my pulse has stopped throbbing
my breath's turned thick
I can't walk straight—
this is an unknown terrain that
my heart's brought me to
look, I am filled up with apprehensions
what is this that my heart has wrought?

I hear somebody call out to me
I turn and find no one
was that my shadow calling out to me
it is only when I drown
that I find myself ashore
what is this that my heart has wrought—
look, the sky's suddenly teeming with stars

देखना मेरे सर से, आसमां उड़ गया है
देखना आसमां के सिरे खुल गए हैं ज़मीं से

देखना क्या हुआ है, ये ज़मीं बह रही है
देखना पानियों में ज़मीं घुल रही है कहीं से
देखना आसमां के सिरे खुल गए हैं ज़मीं से

होश में मैं नहीं, ये गु़शी भी नहीं
इस सदी में कभी ये हुआ ही नहीं

जिस्म घुलने लगा, रूह गलने लगी
पांव रुकने लगे, राह चलने लगी

आसमां बादलों पर कर्वटें ले रहा है
देखना आसमां ही बरसने लगे न ज़मीं पे

ये ज़मीं पानियों में डुबकियां ले रही हैं
देखना उठके पैरों पे चलने लगे न कहीं पे

तुम कहो तो रुकें, तुम कहो तो चलें
ये जुनूं है अगर तो जुनूं सोच लें
तुम कहो तो रुकें, तुम कहो तो चलें
मुझ को पहचानती हैं कहां मंजिलें . . .

behold, the sky has blown off from my head
look, the seams of the sky have come undone at the earth

behold, the earth beneath our feet is drifting
look, somewhere the earth is dissolving in the waters

I am not in my senses
have lost them neither
something like this in this century
hasn't happened either
when bodies blend, and souls begin to melt
when the feet stop
and paths develop feet of their own

the sky's tossing on the clouds
the skies may just rain down on earth
the earth's taking a dip in the waters
it may just grow feet and begin to walk

if you are here, maybe I'll stay
on your say so maybe I'll move ahead
if this be recklessness
so may it be—
these destinations, after all, know not me but you

इस दिल में बसकर देखो तो
ये शहर बड़ा पुराना है

हर सांस में एक कहानी है
हर सांस में इक अफ़साना है
　　ये शहर . . .

ये बस्ती दिल की बस्ती है
कुछ दर्द है, कुछ रुसवाई है
ये कितनी बार उजाड़ी है
ये कितनी बार बसाई है

ये जिस्म है कच्ची मिट्टी का
भर जाए तो रिसने लगता है
बांहों में कोई थामें तो
आग़ोश में गिरने लगता है

come, colonize this heart
this age-old citadel
a fable in each breath
each fabled breath, a story

oft wrecked and oft built
this settlement is that of the heart
a little graced with pain
a little unsettled with disgrace

this body of unbaked clay—
it begins to ooze when it's full
scoop it up in your arms
and it begins to crumble in your embrace

اذکارا

پنجوں کی مہاپیں ہے ا
نیناں مُٹگل لیں گے
پنجوں کی مہاپیں ہے
نیناں مُٹگل لیں گے

طبیعت جاں دو بجھو نلیوں گے
سینہ سپنجر کر دیں گے
نیناں مُٹگل لیں گے

پنجوں کڑو دمنے کاچیسکا اُٹگارہ
نہ پڑ آیا، نہ شنگارہ

پنجوں کا باتوں پہ پورسا نہیں ہُنا
ساری باتاں توانی رے
نیناں مُٹگل لیں گے ....

It's always fun to share poetry with Vishal. He is well groomed in verse, since his father wrote lyrics for films. His father was young then, and Vishal too young.

The folk flavour in this song is in the style of a 'thumri'; that is the charm of this song. The line '*na raseed na khata*' is very unusual to be used in poetry, but working with Vishal, I have been taking these poetic liberties.

I had just missed recording an album with Ustad Nusrat Fateh Ali Khan Saheb, before he left for the USA. That was his last journey—he didn't come back. Recording this song with Rahat, his nephew, was like a token of a blessing for me, left behind by him.

नैनों की मत मानियों रे
नैना ठग लेंगे
नैनों की मत सुनियो रे
नैना ठग लेंगे

जगते जादू फूंकेंगे
नींदें बंजर कर देंगे
भला-मन्दा देखे ना पराया ना सगा रे
नैनों को तो डसने का चस्का लगा रे
नैनों का जहर नशीला रे, बादलों में सतरंगियाँ बोवें
भोर तलक बरसायें
बादलों में सतरंगियाँ बोवें
नैना बावरा कर देंगे
नैना ठग लेंगे . . .

नैना रात को चलते-चलते
स्वर्गाँ में ले जावें
मेघ-मल्हार के सपने बीजें
हरयाली दिखलावें
नैनों की जुबान पे भरोसा नहीं होता
लिखत पढ़त ना रसीद ना खाता
सारी बात हवाई रे
बिण बादल बरसावें सावण
सावण बिण बरसाताँ
बिण बादल बरसावें सावण
नैना बावरा कर देंगे . . .

do not be mesmerized
by the beauty of those eyes—
they will deceive you
do not listen to their promises—
they will blow spells at you
and rob you of your sleep

those eyes do not care
about right or wrong, do not distinguish
between friend and foe
they will sink their fangs into you
infect you with their venom—
and the venom doesn't kill but intoxicates
they plant the clouds with rainbows
and shower you with kaleidoscopic illusions
till the morning's come
they will simply drive you over the edge of sanity

those eyes will show you glimpses of heaven
and all night long, seed your dreams
with fecund possibilities, but—
but it is difficult to believe in the vision
in the assurances those eyes promise
there's no contract, no guarantee
just empty words, hollow promises
of rain under a blistering sun

do not believe those eyes
they are meant to deceive you
merely here to rob you of your sanity

बादलों से काट काट के,
कागज़ों पे नाम जोड़ना
ये मुझे क्या हो गया!

डोरियों से बांध बांध के,
रात भर चांद तोड़ना
ये मुझे क्या हो गया!

एक बार, तुमको जब बरसते पानियों
के पार देखा था
यूँ लगा था जैसे गुनगुनाता एक
आबशार देखा था
तब से मेरी नींद में बरसती रहती हो
बोलती बहुत हो और हंसती रहती हो
जो तुझे जानता न हो
उससे तेरा नाम पूछना
ये मुझे क्या हो गया!

देखो यूँ खुले बदन तुम गुलाबी साहिलों पे आया न करो
नमक भरे समुद्रों में इस तरह नहाया न करो
सारा दिन चांदनी सी छाई रहती है
और गुलाबी धूप बौखलाई रहती है

I shear
the clouds and glue them on paper
to spell your name. Look—
what has come over me!

I string
the moon and keep plucking it
from the stalk of the night
all night long. Look—
what has come over me!

I remember
once, you stood across a sheet of rain
and for a moment I thought
I had seen a waterfall warbling
and ever since, you keep cascading
into my dreams
trilling like a waterfall
and ringing my sleep
with your uninhibited laughter

I ask
complete strangers your name. Look—
what has come over me!

I caution
you not to bare your shoulder on the golden beach
I caution you
not to bathe in the salt-filled seas
lest silvery moonlight permeate the entire day
and golden sunshine keeps seething with rage

जामुनों की नर्म डाल पे,
नाखूनों से नाम खोदना
ये मुझे क्या हो गया . . .

I carve
your name with my nails
on soft trunks of berry trees. Look—
what has come over me!

धागे तोड़ लाओ चांदनी से नूर के
घूंघट ही बनालो रोशनी से नूर के
शर्म आ गई तो
आगोश में लो
सांसों से उलझी रहीं मेरी सांसें
बोलना हलके हलके . . . बोलना हलके हलके . . .

आ नींद का सौदा करें
इक ख़्वाब दे, इक ख़्वाब ले
इक ख़्वाब तो आंखों में है
इक चांद के तकिए तले

कितने दिनों से
ये आसमां भी
सोया नहीं है, उसको सुला दें
बोलना हलके हलके . . . बोलना हलके हलके . . .

उम्रें लगीं कहते हुए
दो लफ़्ज़ थे, इक बात थी
वो एक दिन सौ साल का
सौ साल की वो रात थी
कैसा लगे जो
चुप चाप दोनों
पल पल में पूरी सदियां बिता दें
बोलना हलके हलके . . . बोलना हलके हलके . . .

33 Jhoom Barabar Jhoom (2007)

come!
let's pluck threads of light
from the silvery moon—
and weave the threads
into a veil of light
and perchance if I blush
just pull me in your embrace—
let the weave of my breath
tangle into yours
hush! speak softly!

come!
let's swap our dreams
barter them for sleep:
a dream lingers in your eyes
another snuggles languorously
against the pillow of the moon

look!
the sky hasn't slept for eons
let's sing it a lullaby
hush! speak softly!

it sure took a lifetime
to utter those two words
that single phrase
the day stretched into centuries
and the night was a hundred years long
come!
let the two of us
make these centuries
fleet by in moments
hush! don't say a word!

बोलो क्या तुम बस इतना सा मेरा काम करोगे
मेरे जिस्म पे उंगली से अपना नाम लिखोगे?

आंखों से पढ़ पढ़ के मेरे
जिस्म पे लिखते रहना
सांस बजे गर ज़ोर से कोई
आवाज़ निगलते रहना
हल्की हल्की आंच पे बोलो
ढेर सा प्यार लिखोगे?

हाथों की पोरों से जो भी
तुम महसूस करो
वहां वहां तुम होंठों की एक
मोहर लगाते जाओ
इतना ही चुप चाप बताओ
कितना प्यार करोगे?

बोलो क्या तुम . . .

34 Daayra (1996)

tell me, will you do me a little favour—
will you write
your name
on my body
with your fingertips?

will you keep reading from my eyes
and keep writing on my body
and when the breath
strays from its rhythm
will you put your lips on mine
and swallow its lone voice?
tell me, will you author
a lot of love
on a slow burning flame?

will you seal
the sensations
evoked by your fingertips
with the stamp of your lips
now, come on
quietly, whisper it to me
how much will you love me?

लबों से चूम लो आंखों से थाम लो मुझ को
तुम ही से जन्मूं तो शायद मुझे पनाह मिले . . .

दो सौंधे सौंधे से जिस्म जिस वक़्त
एक मुट्ठी में सो रहे थे
बता तो उस वक़्त मैं कहां था?
बता तो उस वक़्त तू कहां थी?

मैं आरज़ू की तपिश में पिघल रही थी कहीं
तुम्हारे जिस्म से होकर निकल रही थी कहीं
बड़े हसीन थे जो राह में गुनाह मिले . . .
तुम ही से जन्मूं तो . . .

तुम्हारे लब छू के जलने की आरज़ू में
जब अपने ही आपसे लिपटके सुलग रहा था
बता तो उस वक़्त मैं कहां था?
बता तो उस वक़्त तू कहाँ थी?

तुम्हारी आंखों के साहिल से दूर, दूर कहीं
मैं ढूंढ़ती थी मिले ख़ुशबुओं का नूर कहीं
वहीं रुकी हूं जहां से तुम्हारी राह मिले . . .
तुम ही से जन्मूं तो . . .

kiss me with your lips
arrest me with your eyes
only when I am born
out of your womb
will I perhaps find refuge

where was I at the moment when
our two bodies were lying, fragrant
asleep together
where were you then—

somewhere—melting in the swelter of desire
burning my way through your body—
ah! so delectable the bounds of prudence
transgressed on the way—
only when I am born
out of you
will I perhaps find refuge

where was I at the moment when
I embraced myself, smouldering
anticipating the flaming at the touch of your lips
where were you then—

somewhere away,
far away from the shore of your eyes
searching—seeking the blaze of fragrances
but I am still encamped at the place
from where I can find my way
back to you
only when I am born
out of you
will I perhaps find refuge

मैं इस ज़मीं पर भटकता हूं कितना सदियों से
गिरा है वक़्त से कटकर एक लम्हा, उसकी तरह
वतन मिला तो गली के लिए भटकता रहा
गली में घर का निशान ढूंढ़ता रहा बरसों

अब तुम्हारी रूह में, जिस्म में भटकता हूं
तुम ही से जन्मूं तो शायद मुझे पनाह मिले . . .

but I am wandering over this earth, for centuries
fallen, like a moment cleaved from time
when I found a country, I wandered looking for a street
when I found the street, I walked on looking for the sign
of a home—searching on and on for years

and now, I wander in your soul
in your body, still looking—
and only when I am born
out of your womb
will I perhaps find refuge

Do naino mein aansoo bhare hain . . .

This was a 'lori', but when we were recording the music was too loud to give the feel of a lullaby.

I had to request Lataji another day to sing it again with no music. RD was quite apprehensive! But Lataji obliged immediately. She remembered the song.

Hence there is a difference in the two versions of the song, the one used in the film, and the one on the disc.

दो नैनों में
आँसू भरे हैं
निंदिया कैसे समाए

डूबी-डूबी आँखों में सपनों के साए
रात-भर अपने हैं, दिन में पराए

कैसे नैनों में
निंदिया समाए

झूठे तेरे वादों पे बरस बिताए
ज़िंदगी तो काटी, यह रात कट जाए

कैसे नैनों में
निंदिया समाए
दो नैनों में . . .

so filled with tears
the eyes, both
how does sleep slip in?

debris of dreams
floating in drowning eyes
clutch onto them all night long
the day is going to take it all away
how does sleep slip in?

built all these years on your false promises
a lifetime has passed in hope
hope this night passes by

फिर से आइयो—बदरा बिदेसी!
तेरे पंखों पर मोती जड़ूंगी
भर के जाइयो हमारी तलैय्या
मैं तलैय्या किनारे मिलूंगी
तुझे मेरे काली कमली वाले की सौं . . .

फिर से आइयो—बदरा बिदेसी!
तेरे पंखों पर मोती जड़ूंगी

तेरे जाने की रुत मैं जानती हूं
मुड़ के आने की रीत है कि नहीं
काली दर्गाह से पूछूंगी जा के
तेरे मन में भी प्रीत है कि नहीं
कच्ची पुलिया से हो के गुजरियो
कच्ची पुलिया के किनारे मिलूंगी

फिर से आइयो—बदरा बिदेसी!
तेरे पंखों पर मोती जड़ूंगी

तू जो रुक जाऐ मेरी अटरिया
मैं अटरिया पे झालर लगा दूं

डालूं चार ताबीज़ गले में
अपने काजल से बिंदिया लगा दूं

छू के जाइयो हमारी बगीची
मैं पीपल के आड़े मिलूंगी
तुझे मेरे काली कमली वाले की सौं . . .

do come again, o rain-filled clouds—
(you, a stranger to my shores)
I shall string your wings with pearls

fill up our ponds before you go
I shall wait for you by its shores—
swear by my *Kali Kamli Walah* that you will do so

I know the seasons of your leaving
don't you have a tradition of returning
implore I will at *Kali Dargah*
maybe you have some love left for me

do come again, o rain-filled clouds—
pass along that bamboo bridge
I shall wait for you by its edge

if you deign to stop by my terrace
I shall festoon it up with festive lights
I shall put a *tabiz* around it to ward off the evil spirits
even spot it with a *bindiya* from my kohl-lined eyes

drizzle over my orchards before you go
I shall meet you by the peepul tree
swear by my *Kali Kamli Walah* that you will do so

रोज़ अकेली आए
रोज़ अकेली जाए
चांद कटोरा लिए भिखारन रात

मोतियों जैसे तारे
आंचल में हैं सारे
झोली में भर जा भिखारन रात

जोगन जैसी लागे
न सोए न जागे
गली गली में जाए भिखारन रात

रोज़ लगाए फेरा
है कोई नन्हा सबेरा
गोद में भर दो, आई भिखारन रात

38 Mere Apne (1971)

the vagrant night
with the begging bowl
of the moon
tramps in daily

pluck those pearl-like stars
from your *aanchal*
o vagrant night
and pour them in my lap

like an ascetic
neither asleep nor awake
she trolls
from street to street
looking for a new-born dawn
to fill her lap

हरि, दिन तो बीता, शाम हुई, रात पार करा दे
बीता मेरा काल तो बीता, कूल पार करा दे

मैंने साथ लिया न कोई दोशाला न लोई
अपने छूटे, सपने छूटे, आशा और छुड़ा दे

हरि, दिन तो बीता, शाम हुई, रात पार करा दे

दाता, तेरे द्वार खड़ी हूं, मागूं न मोती न दान
बंधु छूटे, बंधन छूटे, छोर पार करा दे

हरि, दिन तो बीता, शाम हुई, रात पार करा दे

the day's gone, evening's come
get me through the night, o Lord!
the river of life I have crossed
the shore's in sight
just bring me ashore, o Lord!

o Lord! I have nothing
to keep me warm anymore—
no friends, no family, nobody to call my own
the aspirations, the dreams are long gone
just help me rid myself of hope too, o Lord!

I stand before you, palms outstretched, o Giver!
beseeching you no more for alms—
the ties with this world are long whittled
just help me float ashore, o Lord!

जां अटकी पई डाल पे, पतझड़ भेजे कोय
प्रीत पके ना धूप से, कैसे कुन्दन होय
रोशनी ही रोशनी, घर जला लिया है
चूल्हा चौखट चौहदा, सब उठा दिया है

जां अटकी थी डाल पे जब झोंका आया
पतझड़ ने दी निजात जो उड़ा दिया है
घर जला लिया है . . .

रात और दिन की टोकरी जो फेंकी सर से
उघड़ा उघड़ा आसमां अब हटा दिया है
घर जला लिया है . . .

my life clings
onto the stalk like a leaf
will someone send for the autumn
for my salvation?

unlike a fruit, love
does not ripen in the sun
unlike gold
the heat does not rid me
of my impurities

for light
I have set my house on fire
burnt my hearth, my home
freed myself of worldly ties
and now that I have flung away
this onerous tote of night and day
off my back, I have
peeled off this sky—
this sky that had already
begun to flake

the autumn blows me
off the stalk, blows me
into salvation

रहमान बिल्कुल एक बोनस की तरह मिला है!

पंचम और उसके बाद विशाल के साथ करते हुये एक तहलीज़ बन गई थी मेरे काम की—और शायरी की। उसमें बड़ा comfortable लग रहा था कि 'दिल से' की आवाज़ आई। उससे पहले एक गाना रहमान के साथ शिवेन्द्र डूंगरपुर के लिये लिख चुका था। लेकिन वो फ़िल्म बंद हो गई थी। 'दिल से' में एक नये अन्दाज़ में गाने लिखने का मौक़ा मिला। मणि रत्नम और रहमान की सूफ़ियाना पसन्द की वजह भी उसमें शामिल थी, उसके अलावा वो रहमान की कम्पोज़ीशन में गाने की एक नई फ़ॉर्म नज़र आई। उस में रिवायती मुखड़ा भी नहीं था, और वो तरतीब कि मुखड़ा, मुखड़े के बाद अंतरा, अंतरे के बाद एक कोरस लाईन, और फिर मुखड़ा . . . ये तरतीब कहीं नहीं थी। रहमान ने गाने को एक आज़ाद नज़्म की शक़्ल दे दी। मेरे लिये दहलीज़ के बाहर क़दम रखने का मौक़ा मिला। पहला ही गाना था 'सतरंगी रे', फिर 'चल छयां छयां', और उसके बाद 'ऐ अजनबी, तू भी कभी आवाज़ दे कहीं से . . .'

103

ऐ अजनबी तू भी कभी
आवाज़ दे कहीं से
मैं यहाँ टुकड़ों में जी रहा हूँ
तू कहीं टुकड़ों में जी रही है

रोज़ रोज़ रेशम सी हवा
आते जाते कहती है बता
वो जो दूध धुली, मासूम कली
वो है कहां कहां
वो रौशनी कहां है
वो जान-सी कहां है
मैं अधूरा, तू अधूरी जी रही है

तू तो नहीं है लेकिन तेरी मुस्कराहटें हैं
चेहरा कहीं नहीं है पर तेरी आहटें हैं
तू है कहां, कहां है, तेरा निशां कहां है
मैं अधूरा, तू अधूरी जी रही है

41 Dil Se (1998)

o stranger
wherever you may be
show me a sign
roll out my name on your tongue

look how I live my life—
in fragments, piecemeal
is your life splintered too?

day in and day out
the silken air brushes against me
and asks
where is she—
that angelic, innocent bud
that glow, that glitter
that breath of your life?
look how incomplete I am—
how incomplete you must be too

you are not here—
yet I see you smile
I do not see your face—
yet I hear your footfall
where may you be—
where is your trail
why must we live—
two incomplete lives?

इस मोड़ से जाते हैं
कुछ सुस्त क़दम रस्ते
कुछ तेज़ क़दम राहें

पत्थर की हवेली को
शीशे के घरौंदों में
तिनकों के नशेमन तक
इस मोड़ से जाते हैं . . .

आंधी की तरह उड़कर
इक राह गुज़रती है
शरमाती हुई कोई
क़दमों से उतरती है

इन रेशमी राहों में
इक राह तो वो होगी
तुम तक जो पहुंचती है
इस मोड़ से जाते हैं . . .

इक दूर से आती है
पास आके पलटती है
इक राह अकेली सी
रुकती है न चलती है

ये सोच के बैठी हूं
इक राह तो वो होगी
तुम तक जो पहुंचती है
इस मोड़ से जाते हैं . . .

from this crossroads spring a number of roads
a few run along at a galloping pace
a few walk on in a leisurely tread

one such road leads to
an imposing mansion of stone
another to a fragile house of glass
and yet another to
a thatched nest of straw

a path swoops down like a tropical storm, suddenly
another descends, blushing, unsure of its next step

I know that amongst these silken roads
there will be a way that leads to you

is that the one—the one in the distance
that suddenly swerves away as it nears
or this—the lonely deserted one
the one that neither moves nor strays

I sit at this bend at the road
trying to fathom which one of these forks
might lead to you

हज़ार राहें मुड़ के देखीं
कहीं से कोई सदा न आई
बड़ी वफ़ा से निभाई तुमने
हमारी थोड़ी सी बेवफ़ाई

जहाँ से तुम मोड़ मुड़ गए थे
ये मोड़ अब भी वहीं पड़े हैं
हम अपने पैरों में जाने कितने
भंवर लपेटे हुए खड़े हैं

कहीं किसी रोज़ यूँ भी होता
हमारी हालत तुम्हारी होती
जो रात हमने गुज़ारी मर के
वो रात तुमने गुज़ारी होती

तुम्हें ये ज़िद थी कि हम बुलाते
हमें ये उम्मीद वो पुकारें
है नाम होंठों पे अब भी लेकिन
आवाज़ में पड़ गई दरारें

हज़ार राहें, मुड़ के देखीं . . .

43 Thodisi Bewafaii (1980)

I turned down a thousand paths
searching, straining to hear your voice
you've reciprocated my little unfaithfulness
with unwavering silence

that bend in the road
where you took a different turn
away from me—is still there
and I . . . am still here
countless vortices
whirled around my feet

how I wish you could
swap a day of my life with yours
then you too could see how
I trudge through every night . . . dying

you were bent on me calling out to you
I hoped you would reach out to me
your name is still on my lips
but my voice . . . fissured

तेरे जाने से तो कुछ बदला नहीं
रात भी आई थी, और चांद भी था
तेरे जाने से तो कुछ बदला नहीं

सांस भी वैसे चलती है, हमेशा की तरह
आंख वैसे ही झपकती है, हमेशा की तरह
थोड़ी सी भीगी हुई रहती है, और कुछ भी नहीं
तेरे जाने से तो कुछ बदला नहीं . . .

होंठ ख़ुश्क होते हैं और प्यास भी लगती है
आज कल शाम ही से सर्द हवा चलती है
बात करने से धुआं उठता है, जो दिल का नहीं
तेरे जाने से तो कुछ बदला नहीं . . .

रात भी आई थी, और चांद भी था
हां मगर
नींद नहीं
नींद नहीं

nothing changed with your going away—
the night too fell
and the moon too came out

my breath is in rhythm, as usual
and my eyes blink, as usual
turn a little moist at times though
—but that's just about it—
nothing changed with your going away

I even feel thirsty
my lips get a little parched
but that's because of the cold winds
that begin to howl at nightfall
and when I try to speak
smoke billows out of my mouth
but, rest assured, this smoke
has nothing to do
with the heart
nothing changed with your going away

the night too fell
and the moon too came out
but—
sleep didn't

तुम गये सब गया, तुम गये सब गया
मैं अपनी ही मिट्टी तले दब गया

कोई आया था कुछ देर पहले यहां
लेके मिट्टी से लीपा हुआ आसमां
क़ब्र पर डाल कर वो गया, कब गया
तुम गये सब गया . . .

हाथों पैरों में तन्हाइयाँ चलती हैं
मेरी आंखों में परछाइयां चलती हैं
एक सैलाब था, सारा घर बह गया
फिर भी जीने का थोड़ा सा डर रह गया
ज़ख्म सीने के क्यों दे गया, जब गया

तुम गये सब गया, तुम गये सब गया
मैं अपनी ही मिट्टी तले दब गया

everything crumbled
when you went away, and
I got buried under the debris
of my own wreck

a while ago, someone
brought a sky
caked with earth
pulled it over my grave
and walked away—
I did not even realize when

a loneliness trolls
my hands and feet
and shadows tramp
my eyes

a tornado swooped down on my house
scooped away everything
but left behind
a little fear—of living

why did you leave behind a wound
in my bosom when you went away?

This song has a very special place in my memory. It was from my second film and my first with R.D. Burman.

When I was picturizing the song, Ravi (Jeetendra) reacted to the song with apprehension. He was not sure of its melody or the verse. He expressed his doubts very mildly, though he was the producer too.

In the lunch break he took Amit (Amitabh Bachchan) with him and played the song to him. Maybe Amit was passing through some emotional crisis. There were tears in his eyes as the song ended. And Ravi's smile came back.

The song remained intact. In course of time, it brought the National Award for Lataji—and I think Bhupi too: I will check up!

बीती न बिताई रैना
बिरहा की जाई रैना
भीगी हुई अँखियों ने
लाख बुझाई रैना

बीती हुई बतियाँ कोई दोहराए
भूले हुए नामों से कोई तो बुलाए

चाँद की बिंदी वाली
बिंदी वाली रतियाँ
जागी हुई अंखियों में
रात न आई रैना

युग आते हैं और युग जाए
छोटी छोटी यादों के पल नहीं जाए

झूठ से काली लागे, लागे काली रतियां
रूठी हुई अंखियों ने लाख मनाई रैना
बीती न बिताई रैना . . .

this night
—born of separation—
does not sink
however hard I try
to drown it
in tear-filled eyes

I yearn
for someone—
to recount
those old familiar moments
to call me
by long-forgotten names

the moon's a *bindi*
on the forehead of the night
reminiscent of all those other nights
the night refuses to descend
in these wakeful eyes, tonight

time ages
and an age fades away
but memories
of small little moments
stretch—
into eternity

the night
becomes blacker
than lies—
refuses to be pacified

बड़ी देर से मेघा बरसा ओ रामा
जली कितनी रतियां . . .

इस पहलू झुलसी, तो उस पहलू सोयी
सारी रात सुलगी मैं, आया न कोई . . .
बैठी रही रखके हथेली पे दो अँखियां
जागी सारी रतियां . . .

थोड़ा सा तेज़ कभी, थोड़ा सा हल्का
रोका न जाए मुई आँखियों का टपका
लाखों पिरोई मैंने मोतियों की लड़ियाँ
जागी सारी रतियां . . .

बड़ी देर से मेघा बरसा ओ रामा
जली कितनी रतियां . . .

it sure took a long time to rain, o Rama
countless nights did I burn

I blistered at times on this side
tried to steal a few winks on the other
the whole night I smouldered
waiting with my eyes resting on my palms
but nothing stirred, nobody came

the eyes rained, at times drizzled
the tears would just never ebb
lakhs of pearls I twirled into a string
but the night couldn't be strung away

it sure took a long time to rain, o Rama
countless nights did I burn

सुरमई शाम इस तरह आए
साँस लेते हैं जिस तरह साए

कोई आहट नहीं बदन की कहीं
फिर भी लगता है तू यहीं है कहीं
वक़्त जाता सुनाई देता है
तेरा साया दिखाई देता है
जैसे ख़ुश्बू नज़र से छू जाए
सुरमई शाम इस तरह आए . . .

दिन का जो भी पहर गुज़रता है
कोई एहसान सा उतरता है
वक़्त के पाँव देखता हूं मैं
रोज़ ये छाँव देखता हूं मैं
आए जैसे कोई ख़्याल आए
सुरमई शाम इस तरह आए . . .

the grey evening
creeps in
and the shadows start breathing

no footfall
not even a whisper of your presence
and yet I feel you're here—
somewhere

I hear time fleeing
I see your presence
silhouetted
like invisible fragrance brushing the eyes

a load heaves off the heart
as the sun goes down
I see the feet of Time
cast a shadow
loom in like a thought

ख़ाली हाथ शाम आई है
ख़ाली हाथ जाएगी

आज भी ना आया कोई
ख़ाली लौट जाएगी

आज भी ना आए आँसू
आज भी न भीगे नैना
आज भी ये कोरी रैना
कोरी लौट जाएगी

रात की स्याही कोई
आए तो मिटाए ना
आज ना मिटाई तो ये
कल भी लौट आएगी
ख़ाली हाथ शाम आई है . . .

the evening's come empty-handed
and empty-handed it will return

tonight too, no one has come
tonight too, the tears stay away
tonight too, the eyes are parched
tonight too, the barren night will stay
uninked, blank

someone must come
and wipe the blackness
of this night
or else
this black night
will come back again
and again

मेरे सरहाने जलाओ सपने
मुझे जरा-सी तो नींद आए

ख़याल चलते हैं आगे-आगे
मैं उनकी छाँव में चल रही हूँ
ना जाने किस मोम से बनी हूँ
जो क़तरा-क़तरा पिघल रही हूँ
मैं सहमी रहती हूँ नींद में भी
कहीं कोई ख़्वाब डस ना जाए

कभी बुलाता है कोई साया
कभी उड़ाती है धूल कोई
मैं एक भटकी हुई-सी ख़ुश्बू
तलाश करती हूँ फूल कोई
जरा किसी शाख़ पर तो बैठूँ
जरा तो मुझको हवा झुलाए

50 Maya Memsaab (1993)

light up my dreams by the side of my pillow
let me snatch a few winks of sleep at least

my fears race ahead of me and
I'm walking forever in their shadows
what kind of wax is this that I'm made of
that I melt drop by drop
I stay awake—even in my sleep
lest a dream sink its fangs into me

at times bewitched by shadows
and at others whirled by the dust
I am but a disembodied fragrance
searching for a flower—
wish I could roost a little time on a tree branch
a little time I wish I could sway in the breeze

No Sparking.

رات سے آدھی رات بھی ہوئی ان گھر کے پاس میں

بیٹھ سے آدھی رات بھی تم راتیں گھر بیٹھی ہیں

یہ الیکش کمر مبرش جاریں ہے ......

یہ کسی ٹھکر کو سیکھے پکڑ کر

مشنگ ہے میں

یہ اسلے سے نبری ......

حقواں چیتا ہے بازیگر کی طرح بواس

معیل شیل سکاتا اور رہی

کوئی کر تب دکھا رہی ہے

یہ الیکش کمر مبرش ....

اکیل اس

Bahut se aadhey bujhey huye din pade hain

No Smoking was a rare experience. Firstly I could not understand the story when I read the script. But there was something attractive about it. It was like a dream, which you can't understand, or interpret, but it was there. Anurag Kashyap, the director, had weird images, which he portrayed on the screen successfully. Some he could explain, some he couldn't.

Since the songs were not lip-synched, we decided to approach them the other way. He would give me the sequence where he wanted the song, and I would write accordingly.

Ultimately *No Smoking* touched a high mark poetically in my lyric-writing.

Unfortunately the words were drowned in the heavy noise of the orchestra, and made no difference to the film.

बहुत से आधे बुझे हुए दिन पड़े हैं इसमें
बहुत सी आधी जली हुई रातें गिर पड़ी हैं
ये ऐश-ट्रे भरती जा रही है

कि सूखे टुकड़े हैं कुछ तलब के
सुलग रहे हैं, सुलग रहे हैं
ये ऐश-ट्रे भरती जा रही है

धुआं लिपटता है बाज़ीगर की तरह हवा से
वो पलटे, बल खाके उठ रहा है
तमाम करतब दिखा रहा है
ये ऐश-ट्रे भरती जा रही है

न हाथ डालो
कि वक़्त से छीले हुए लम्हों की राख गर्म है
उंगलियां जलेंगी
ये ऐश-ट्रे भरती जा रही है

this ashtray is fast filling up with
umpteen stubs of days, still smouldering
and numerous butts of nights, partially burnt

these ruddy stumps are of fleeting moments
still fuming
this ashtray is fast filling up

the smoke clings onto the air
like an acrobat
swinging mid-air
strutting a new feat
this ashtray is fast filling up

don't pick the ashtray up
for the ash
of the moments shredded from time
is still smouldering—
you will only scorch your fingertips

this ashtray is fast filling up

धीरे जलना, धीरे जलना
जिंदगी की लौ पे जलना

कांच का सपना गल ही ना जाये
सोच समझ के आँच रखना
धीरे जलना . . .

होना है जो होना है वो
होने से तो रुकता नहीं
आसमां तो झुकता नहीं
धीरे जलना . . .

तेरे रूप की हल्की धूप में
दो ही पल हैं, जीने हैं
तेरी आँख में, देख चुका हूं
वो सपने हैं, सीने हैं
आँखों में सपनों की किरचें हैं,
चुभतीं हैं
धीरे जलना . . .

सोचा ना था जिंदगी ऐसे
फिर से मिलेगी जीने के लिये
आँखों को, प्यास लगेगी
अपने ही आँसू पीने के लिये

धीरे धीरे, धीरे जलना
जिंदगी की लौ पे जलना

flare up slowly
on the flame of life

this dream of glass
it may melt
be careful when you raise the blaze of life—
flare it up slowly
what is destined to happen
is wont to happen
it cannot be stopped from happening
the sky doesn't bend at will

in the mellowed sun of your presence
I've but only a few moments to live
when I peep into your eyes
I see tatters of dreams
I need to stitch them together—
pick out those shards of dreams
lacerating your eyes

flare up slowly
on the flame of life

hadn't thought
I would get another chance
to live life
hadn't thought
that these eyes of mine
would thirst after their own tears

flare up slowly
on this flame of life

शाम से आँख में नमी सी है
आज फिर आपकी कमी सी है

दफ़्न कर दो हमें कि साँस मिले
नब्ज़ कुछ देर से थमी सी है

वक़्त रुकता नहीं कहीं टिककर
इसकी आदत भी आदमी सी है

कोई रिश्ता नहीं रहा फिर भी
एक तसलीम लाज़मी सी है

53 Marasim (1993)

there's a dampness in my eyes
since the evening has set
I feel your absence once again
today

bury me
so that I may catch my breath
my pulse has stopped throbbing
for quite some time

time does not stand still
at one place
it too has picked up
the habits of humans

agreed there's nothing left
between the two of us
but shouldn't we at least exchange greetings
when we chance upon one another?

फिर वही रात है
रात है ख़्वाब की
रात भर ख़्वाब में
देखा करेंगे तुम्हें
फिर वही रात है
रात है ख़्वाब की

मासूम-सी नींद में
जब कोई सपना चले
हमको बुला लेना तुम
पलकों के पर्दे तले

ये रात है ख़्वाब की, ख़्वाब की रात है
फिर वही रात है

काँच के ख़्वाब हैं
आँखों में चुभ जाएँगे
पलकों में लेना इन्हें
आँखों में रुक जाएँगे

यह रात है ख़्वाब की
फिर वही रात है
रात है ख़्वाब की
रात भर ख़्वाब में
देखा करेंगे तुम्हें

once again the night returns
the night of dreams
I'll be seeing you—

in that innocent sleep of yours
when a dream begins to run
call me over behind the curtains
of your eyelids
but careful—
these dreams are made of glass
they may pierce your eyes
usher them in
on the cushion of your lashes
maybe then they will stay
unbroken in your eyes

once again the night returns . . .
once again I'll be seeing you . . .

पलकों पे चलते चलते जब ऊंघने लगती हैं
सोजा, आंखें सोती हैं तो उड़ने लगती हैं
सौंधे से आकाश पे नीले बजरे बहते हैं
पाखी जैसी आंखें सपने चुगने लगती हैं

पिघली हुई है गीली चाँदनी
कच्ची रात का सपना आए
थोड़ी सी जागी थोड़ी सी सोई
नींद में कोई अपना आए
नींद में हल्की ख़ुशबूएं सी घुलने लगती है
पलकों पे चलते चलते . . .

आंखों से कहना लोरी में बहना
रातों का कोई छोर नहीं
तेरे तो और भी होंगे सपने
मेरा तो कोई और नहीं
ओढ़ के आंखें नींद में सपने सुनने लगती है
पलकों पे चलते चलते . . .

when the long walk on the eyelids makes
you drowsy—sleep, o ye eyes, sleep!

and when the eyes sleep, they
clip on their wings and fly where
blue-canopied barges are adrift on a fragrant sky
and bird-like eyes begin to peck on dreams

the damp moon's molten on a silvery spread
the night's still young on its dreamy thread
and when in that part-awake, part-asleep state
somebody I call my own
walks into my dream—
a hint of delicate fragrances then
begins to melt into my sleep

tell the eyes to flow out in lullabies
for the nights have no ends
you may have many more dreams to cling on to
but for me there is one, just this one

and sleep pulls the wraps of my eyes snug
and begins to listen to my this one dream

55 Panga (1996)

فی الحال

اے زندگی ... پہلے جو لینے دے
پلکیں لکھا
کچھ بہت نہیں
اوّر بنا کچھ سے لکھنے دے
جو بھی لکھا ہے — دل سے لکھا ہے
پہلے — فی الحال جو لینے دے

معصوم سی ہنسی ، بے غرضی سی بھی
موشگوف یہ کھیل جاتی ہے —
انجان سی خوش بخش برستی لکھیں
ساحل سے مل جاتی ہے :
یو انجان دُور ، اجنبیا سے مگر
خوشبوش سے جو لینے دے
پلکھ فی الحال
. . . . .

इस गाने का क्रैडिट मैं मेघना को देता हूं। वो डायरेक्टर थी इस फ़िल्म की—और फ़िल्म का टाइटल 'फ़िलहाल' मुझे शायरी में अच्छा नहीं लग रहा था। मैंने गाना कई तरह से लिखा। सिचुएशन भी बहुत साफ़ नहीं लग रही थी। लेकिन ये गाना उसके ज़हन में था जो वो बयान नहीं कर पा रही थी। आख़िरकार उसने पूरी तफ़सील (detail) अपने ख़्याल की, अंग्रेज़ी में मुझे दे दी।

तर्ज़ वो पहले ही तय कर चुकी थी अन्नु मलिक के साथ! मैंने लिख तो दिया, लेकिन फिर भी पूरी तसल्ली नहीं हुई—तसल्ली तब जाकर हुई जब वो गाना चल निकला और आज तक लोग उसका हवाला देते हैं। लेकिन इसके मिसरे (verses) आज भी मुझे शायरी (poetry) और नसर (prose) के बीच में लटके हुये लगते हैं!

ज़िन्दगी—ये लम्हा जी लेने दे
पहले से लिखा
कुछ भी नहीं
रोज़ नया कुछ
लिखती है तू
जो भी लिखा है दिल से जीया है
ये लम्हा फ़िलहाल जी लेने दे . . .

मासूम सी हंसी बेवजह ही कभी
होंठों पे खिल जाती है
अनजान सी ख़ुशी बहती हुई कभी
साहिल पे मिल जाती है
ये अनजाना डर, अजनबी है मगर
ख़ूबसूरत है, ये लम्हा जी लेने दे
ये लम्हा फ़िलहाल जी लेने दे . . .

दिल ही में रहता है, आंखों में बहता है
कच्चा सा एक ख़्वाब है
लगता सवाल है, शायद जवाब है
दिल फिर भी बेताब है
ये सुकूँ है तो है, ये जुनूँ है तो है
ख़ूबसूरत है, जी लेने दे
ये लम्हा फ़िलहाल जी लेने दे . . .

पहले से लिखा
कुछ भी नहीं
रोज़ नया कुछ
लिखती है तू
ख़ूबसूरत है, जी लेने दे
ये लम्हा फ़िलहाल जी लेने दे

o life!
you have not pre-ordained
anything
each day you author
something afresh
and whatever you have decreed
I have lived it faithfully

but for now
let me live this moment
in which—
a cherubic smile stretches the lips without any reason
an obscure happiness buoys up on the shore
the unexplored may hold a fear
and yet is appealingly beautiful
just let me live this moment

a nascent dream
hidden in the heart
suddenly surfaces in the eyes at times—
and asks a lot of questions
answering them itself
in quick succession
the heart knows no quiet:
if this be happiness so be it
if this be madness so be it
whatever it may be—
it is beautiful
let me just live it, live in it
at least for now

एक सुबह इक मोड़ पर . . .
मैंने कहा उसे रोक कर
हाथ बढ़ा ए ज़िन्दगी
आंख मिला के बात कर

रोज़ तेरे जीने के लिए,
इक सुबह मुझे मिल जाती है
मुरझाती है कोई शाम अगर,
तो रात कोई खिल जाती है
मैं रोज़ सुबह तक आता हूं
और रोज़ शुरू करता हूं सफ़र

तेरे हज़ारों चेहरों में
एक चेहरा है, मुझ से मिलता है
आंखों का रंग भी एक सा है
आवाज़ का अंग भी मिलता है
सच पूछो तो हम दो जुड़वां हैं
तू शाम मेरी, मैं तेरी सहर

रोज़ सुबह इक मोड़ पर . . .

one morning, around a bend in the road
I stopped Life, and said
reach out to me—
look me in the eyes and talk to me

each day for me to live
I am given a morning
and when an evening wilts
a night blossoms
each day I arrive at the morning
and each day I begin a fresh journey

and amongst your thousand faces
there's a face that resembles mine—
our eyes are of the same colour
and our voices sound the same

(and Life said:)
if truth be told, you and I
are each other's twin
you are my dusk
I am your dawn

अजनबी शहर है, अजनबी शाम है
ज़िन्दगी, अजनबी, क्या तेरा नाम है
अजीब है ये ज़िन्दगी, ये ज़िन्दगी अजीब है
ये मिलती है, बिछड़ती है, बिछड़ के फिर से मिलती है

आपके बग़ैर भी हमें
मीठी लगीं उदासियाँ
क्या! ये आपका . . . आपका, कमाल है
शायद आपको ख़बर नहीं
हिल रही है पांव की ज़मीं
क्या! ये आपका . . . आपका, ख़्याल है

अजनबी शहर में
ज़िन्दगी मिल गई

अजीब है ये ज़िन्दगी, ये ज़िन्दगी अजीब है
मैं समझा था क़रीब है, ये और का नसीब है
अजनबी शहर में . . .

बात है ये एक रात की
आप बादलों पे लेटे थे
वो याद है, आप ने बुलाया था

सर्दी लग रही थी आपको
पतली चांदनी लपेटे थे
और शाल में, ख़्वाब के सुलाया था

I meet Life, the perpetual stranger, once again
on a quaint evening in a strange city
Life—stranger—won't you tell me your name?
or will you stay forever a stranger to me
bumping into me one moment, running away the next
only to scamper back into my embrace again?

you are nowhere around, and yet
I find a cheeriness in this melancholy—
or is this the magic woven by your wand?
perhaps you are not aware
the ground beneath the feet is quivering
or is this just the thought of you?

I have found Life
in a strange city
the life that I had thought
always within my grasp, but
destined to be another's
it is strange, this life—

do you remember that night
you were propped up against a cushion of clouds
and you had rolled my name off your lips
you were a little chilly, wrapped in
a gossamer of moonlight, remember—
I had tucked you warm
in the shawl of my thoughts

strange those moments may seem
but they are stitched onto my breath

अजनबी, ही सही, सांस में सिल गई . . .
अजीब है ये ज़िन्दगी, ये ज़िन्दगी अजीब है
मेरी नहीं ये ज़िन्दगी, रक़ीब का नसीब है
अजनबी शहर में . . .

it is strange, this thing called life
not mine, even this life
perhaps it belongs to
my rival for your love

छूटे नाहीं छूटे ना, छूटे नाहीं छूटे ना
रेशम की डोरियों से मनवा ने बांधा है
माटी का ये चोला छूटे ना
साँस का ये तागा बैरी

दाँत से न काटा जाए
पानी से गले न माटी
जितना भी रौंदा जाए
मोह की गिरह लागी
माया तेरा भोला छूटे ना . . .

बहती नदी में हाय
तू बिन तर जाए कोई
कामना का अंगारा ले
कैसे घर जाए कोई
कौड़ी कौड़ी जोड़ी मौला
नातों का ये झोला छूटे ना
छूटे नाहीं छूटे ना . . .

it's not easy to cast off life
not easy to snip these threads of silk
that the soul winds around this body of clay

not easy to clip
this cursed thread of breath
this clay—
you cannot gnaw at it with your teeth
it refuses to be eroded by water
the more you trample upon it
the more enticing its illusions become
and the sturdier the knots of its attachments

how can I
cross a river in spate
without getting wet
how do you expect me
to come to you
with the embers of desire
still burning my soul?

this quilt of life
that I have patched together
kin by kin, friend by friend
is not easy to cast off, o Maula

ओ मांझी रे
अपना किनारा
नदिया की धारा है

साहिलों पे बहने वाले कभी सुना तो होगा कहीं
काग़ज़ों की कश्तियों का कोई किनारा होता नहीं

कोई किनारा जो किनारे से मिले,
वो अपना किनारा है
ओ मांझी रे . . .

पानियों में बह रहे हैं कई किनारे टूटे हुए
रास्तों में मिल गए हैं सभी सहारे छूटे हुए

कोई सहारा मंझधार में मिले तो
अपना सहारा है
ओ मांझी रे . . .

sail me, o boatman
into the middle of the river
for the midstream
is my destination

have any of you
harboured in the comfort of the shore
heard sometimes, somewhere
that paper boats find no moorings, no shores

sail me, o boatman
to the place where
the two shores meet
midstream

battered shores cleaved
from the river banks
float in the stream—
the stilts and the supports
flotsams of life all
bob along my sail

but will I find
a wind in my sail
when I'm midstream
a support, perhaps?

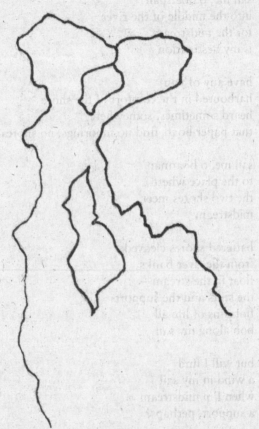

In the ruins of Mandu, the walls of bricks and bodies have fallen, but the love of Baaz Bahadur and Roopmati has survived.

I find it a fascinating haunt. While driving from Bombay to northern India, Mandu was always my favourite place to halt for the night.

Though Mandu has fallen prey to noisy touristy attractions in recent times, the ruins still haunt me as a lovers' rendezvous. When I was writing this song, the location was very much alive in my mind. Later I picturized it there.

नाम गुम जाएगा, चेहरा ये बदल जाएगा
मेरी आवाज़ ही पहचान है, गर याद रहे

वक़्त के सितम कम हसीं नहीं
आज है यहाँ कल कहीं नहीं
वक़्त से परे अगर मिल गए कहीं
मेरी आवाज़ ही पहचान है गर याद रहे . . .

जो गुज़र गई, कल की बात थी
उम्र तो नहीं, एक रात थी
रात का सिरा, अगर फिर मिले कहीं
मेरी आवाज़ ही पहचान है गर याद रहे . . .

दिन ढले जहाँ, रात पास हो
ज़िन्दगी की लौ, ऊँची कर चलो
याद आए गर कभी, जी उदास हो
मेरी आवाज़ ही पहचान है गर याद रहे . . .

the name will fade away
the face will alter
my voice is my only identity
if you remember

the tyrannies of time
are no less charming
alive one moment
obliterated the next
and perchance if we meet
beyond the vagaries of time
remember—
my voice is my only identity

you and I
are in the past now, spent
the span of just one night
not a lifetime
and if you ever stumble across
that lost strand of the night
remember—
my voice is my only identity

when day fades
and the night is nigh—
walk with the wick of life
raised a little high
perchance if you think of me
and sadness gnaws at your heart
remember—
my voice is my only identity

जब कभी मुड़ के देखता हूँ मैं
तुम भी कुछ अजनबी सी लगती हो
मैं भी कुछ अजनबी सा लगता हूं

साथ ही साथ, चलते चलते कहीं
हाथ छूटे मगर, पता ही नहीं
आँसुओं से भरी सी आंखों में
डूबी डूबी हुई सी लगती हो
तुम बहुत अजनबी सी लगती हो

हम जहाँ थे वहाँ पे अब तो नहीं
पास रहने का कोई सबब तो नहीं
कोई नाराज़गी भी नहीं है, मगर
फिर भी रूठी हुई सी लगती हो

रात उदास नज़्म लगती है
ज़िन्दगी सिर्फ़ रस्म लगती है
एक बीते हुए से रिश्ते की
एक बीती घड़ी से लगते हो . . .

तुम भी जब अजनबी से लगते हो
जब कभी मुड़ के देखती हूं मैं
तुम भी कुछ अजनबी से लगते हो

whenever I turn back and look
you appear a bit of a stranger
a bit of a stranger, I too

I do not remember when
in this—our walk together
we let go of each other's hands
and now—when in these eyes brimming with tears
I find you drowning
you appear such a stranger

we are not where we used to be once
there's not even an excuse
a reason to be together any more
no unpleasantness between us, but
yet you appear unhappy

the night's a melancholic dirge
life a mere ritual
and you—
a spent moment
in a spent relationship

ख़ामोश सा अफ़साना
पानी से लिखा होता
ना तुमने कहा होता
ना हमने सुना होता

दिल की बात ना पूछो
दिल तो आता रहेगा
दिल बहकाता रहा है
दिल बहकाता रहेगा
दिल को तुम ने
कुछ तो समझाया होता

सहमे से रहते हैं
जब ये दिन ढलता है
एक दिया बुझता है
एक दिया जलता है
तुम ने कोई तो
दीप जलाया होता

63 Libaas (1988)

you should have
scribbled our unvoiced tale
in water
unarticulated
on your lips
inaudible
to my ears

you should have
taught this conjurer heart
something, unbridled
it always
whips up
yet another illusion

uneasiness creeps in
as the night falls
a hope, doused
a lamp, illuminated
you should have
lit a ray
of hope

समय और धीरे चलो
बुझ गए राह से छाँव
दूर है पी का गाँव
धीरे चलो . . .

जी को बहला लिया
तू ने आस निराश का खेल किया
चार दिनों में कोई, जिया न जिया
ज़हर ये सांस का पिया न पिया

ये हवा सब ले गई
कारवां के निशां भी उड़ा ले गई
उड़ती हवाओं वाले मिलेंगे कहाँ
कोई बता दो पिया का निशां

समय और धीरे चलो
बुझ गए राह से छाँव . . .

64 Rudaali (1993)

slow down o Time, slow down a little more
the sun has stifled the shades from the road
and the home of my beloved is still afar

you amuse yourself, o Time
watching us etch a life
in the handful of time allotted
slow down, o Time—
you have played far too long
this game of hope and despair
slow down—
must we breathe, must we live?

the winds of time
have swept away everything
even the signs of the caravan that went by
where will I now find those
gone with the wind
show me, o Time
the traces of my beloved

slow down o Time, slow down

दौड़ा दौड़ा, भागा भागा सा
वक़्त ये सख़्त है
थोड़ा थोड़ा, माँगा माँगा सा

तुड्डा खाके दिन गिरा, रात ने उठा लिया
हाथ पांव पोंछ के, ताक़ पे बिठा दिया
चाँद का चराग़ है, खूँटियों पे टाँगा
टाँगा टाँगा सा
थोड़ा थोड़ा, माँगा माँगा सा

टिकटिकाती सुइयां, घड़ी की रुकती ही नहीं
रस्सियां ये वक़्त की, गले से खुलती ही नहीं

जिस्म का लिबास है
चीरा चीरा
चीरा चीरा, धागा धागा सा
थोड़ा थोड़ा, माँगा माँगा सा

वक़्त ये सख़्त है . . .

time is on the run
you huff and you puff
to catch up with it
but it's on the run
breathless, panting
always on the run
this time is a little hard on you, eh!
a little borrowed, not even your own, eh?

over there, look—the day has stumbled
see—time has fallen flat on its chin
run—catch up with it
but what's this—
the night has already picked it up
licked its wounds clean
and put it back up on the shelf
now time lights the lamp of the moon
dangles it in your face
run, catch up with it
if you can

now, how you wish
the hands of your watch would stop ticking
how you wish
the noose of time would be taken off your neck
but that is not to be
this time will always be hard on you
for this body of yours
is but a robe—tattered, threadbare—
borrowed from
time itself

غلام علی

دلِ مائلِ مستی کن بروخش،

بہار ہجراں بہار دل ہے

شنائے دیتے ہم جی کو خون کن

تمہارا دل یا ہمارا دل ہے

وقت کے بلو میں ایسے بیٹھے

کہ شاخ گلشن پہ نئی پتی ہے

ذرا سی ہنسی کہی طبیعت،

ذرا سی ہلکن بوگن ہے

کسے کہیں شاخِ الپ جھمکلش ہے جیسے گلِ آتری مہیں

شورہ سینے سے پھٹتا دھواں سا بادل دل سے اُٹھ رہے ہے

پھر لبوں پہ آپ چھایا ہے کتاب،

نظر رکھ تے میں چنگل گئی ہے

تمہاری پگلی سے میری چشمم

سدھار یار آنکھوں میں گلی ہے

Laxmikant was a bubbly man, who composed some very sober tunes. His other half, Pyarelal, is a very sober man, who composed very bubbly music. I had just a few chances of working with them, and *Ghulami* was one of those few opportunities.

There was a song for a group of gypsies to sing in the film. It was a very general situation for a very general song, and the director was open to any suggestion. Laxmikant had composed a tune based on 'kehmukranian' of Amir Khusrau, a thirteenth century poet, where the first line would run in Persian, and the next in Avadhi.

He played the song:

ज़िहाले मिस्कीं मकुन तग़ाफ़ुल, वराये नैनां बनाये बत्तियां
कि क़ल्बे हिजरां नदारम अए जां, न ले हो काहे लगाये छत्तियां।

The director liked the tune but he was not keen on Persian—and Laxmikant was very keen to keep the opening phrase as it was.

So I managed both:

ज़िहाले मिस्कीं मकुन बरंजिश
बहाले हिजरां बेचारा दिल है।

जिहाले मिस्कीं मकुन बरंजिश
बहाले हिजरां बेचारा दिल है
सुनाई देती है जिसकी धड़कन
तुम्हारा दिल या हमारा दिल है

वो आ के पहलू में ऐसे बैठे
कि शाम रंगीन हो गई है
ज़रा ज़रा सी खिली तबियत
ज़रा सी ग़मगीन हो गई है

कभी कभी शाम ऐसे ढलती है
जैसे घूंघट उतर रहा है
तुम्हारे सीने से उठता धुआँ
हमारे दिल से गुज़र रहा है

ये शर्म है, या हया है, क्या है
नज़र उठाते ही झुक गई है
तुम्हारी पलकों से गिर के शबनम
हमारी आँखों में रुक गई है

must you look
at my wretched heart
with so much anguish
have pity—
this heart of mine is raw
from the wounds of separation
but tell me, this pounding that I hear
is this your heart beating or mine?

the way you come and sit
in the shadow of my embrace
this darkness of the evening
is illuminated
the heart soars a little
and sinks a little

there are times when
the evening reveals the night
like a veil coming off
and the breath
that rises in your bosom
finds its way into me
traversing through my heart

is this shyness, or coyness
what may this be
that you lower your eyes
the moment they meet mine
look, that drop of dew on your lashes
has rolled and found a home—in mine

तू मेरे रू–ब–रू है
मेरी आँखों की इबादत है
ये ज़मीं हैं मुहब्बत की
यहां मना है ख़ता करना
सिर्फ़ सजदे में गिरना है
और अदब से दुआ करना

तू मेरे रू–ब–रू है
बस इतनी इजाज़त दे
कदमों में जबीं रख दूँ
फिर सर ना उठे मेरा
ये जाँ भी वहीं रख दूँ

इक बार तो दीदार दे
मेरे सामने रह के भी तू
ओझल है तू
पोशिदा है
मेरे हाल से ख़्वाबीदा है

रू–ब–रू पिया
खू ब रू पिया

you and I face each other
and my eyes read you, silently
like hymns from a prayer book

this place where you stand
is a shrine to love
all thoughts of impropriety banished
all you are allowed to do here
is fall on your knees: genuflect
pray reverentially

now that you grace me
with your presence
pray allow me
to prostrate myself at your feet
allow me to give up my life
so that this head of mine
stays bowed at your feet

but o beautiful beloved of mine
even though you are face to face with me
you are still invisible, hidden
unaware of my plight

come, reveal yourself
show me your glimpse, once
just once

एक मासूम सी दिल की तजवीज़ है
इश्क में जान दे दे . . . बड़ी चीज़ है
दीवाना बना अपना
दीवानगी यूँ भी है
पैरों में पड़ी गर्दिश
और सर में जुनूँ भी है
इस बार तो दीदार दे
जाँ वार दे

गर तू नहीं तो ये ज़िन्दगी
कुछ भी नहीं कुछ भी नहीं
ये बंदगी कुछ भी नहीं . . . कुछ भी नहीं
ये ज़िन्दगी कुछ भी नहीं

this innocent heart of mine suggests
come, lose yourself in love
there's much joy in it
come, craze me in your love
the insanity already exists
look at the whirlpools at my feet
the frenzy in my head
come bestow a meaning upon this lunacy

come now, this once
show me your glimpse
for this one glimpse
I'll entrust my life to you
pledge it all away
for without you, this life is futile
and this devotion meaningless

come, reveal yourself to me
let my eyes read you, silently
like hymns from a prayer book

दिल का रसिया और कहाँ होगा
इश्क़ की आग का धुआँ जहाँ होगा

पीड़ा पाले ग़म सहलाए
कैसे कैसे जी बहलाए
बावरा है, भला माना कहाँ होगा . . .

रूखे सूखे तिनके रखना
फूँकना और चिंगारियां चखना
भोगी है जोगी ये, चैन कहाँ होगा . . .

68 Vaada (2000)

where else will you find
the follower of the heart
but by the smoke
rising from the fire
of love?

he nurses pain
caresses cheerlessness
and fashions strange ways
to amuse himself

he is insane—
how will he be
hale and hearty?
he is an ascetic
his only possession
a few dry twigs of love
with which he stokes
the fire
savouring the flying sparks

this ascetic is
a hedonist too—
how will he be
at peace with himself?

तुम पुकार लो, तुम्हारा इन्तज़ार है
ख़्वाब चुन रही है रात, बेक़रार है

होंठ पे लिये हुए दिल की बात हम
जागते रहेंगे और कितनी रात हम

मुख़्तसर सी बात है तुमसे प्यार है
. . . तुम्हारा इन्तज़ार है

दिल बहल तो जाएगा इस ख़्याल से
हाल मिल गया तुम्हारा अपने हाल से

रात ये क़रार की बेक़रार है
. . . तुम्हारा इन्तज़ार है

I stay awake nights
in hope that you will call me
the night passes in restlessness
gleaning along countless dreams

the secrets of the heart
can no longer be reined in on my lips
how many more nights
must these sleep-bereft eyes
stay awake

a small matter
of a few simple words—
I am in love with you . . .
and, I'm waiting—
for you

the heart is consoled by the thought
that your feelings resemble my lot
and this night of promises—
when my longing is to be laid to rest—
is restless
waiting—
for you

दोस्तों से झूठी मूठी दूसरों का नाम लेके फिर मेरी बातें करना
यारा रात से दिन करना
लम्बी जुदाई तेरी, बड़ा मुश्किल है आहों से दिल भरना
यारा रात से दिन करना
कब ये पूरी होगी, दूर ये दूरी होगी, रोज़ सफ़र करना
यारा रात से दिन करना

चुपके से, चुपके से रात की चादर तले
चांद को भी आहट ना हो, बादल के पीछे चलें
जलें क़तरा क़तरा
गलें क़तरा क़तरा
रात भी न हिले आधी आधी
रात भी ना हिले
चुपके से, चुपके से रात की चादर तले

फरवरी की सर्दियों की धूप में
मूंदी मूंदी आंखियों से देखना, हाथ की आड़ से
नीमि-नीमि ठंड, और आग में
हौले हौले मारवा के राग में
'मीर' की बात हो

दिन भी न डूबे, रात न आये, शाम कभी न ढले
शाम ढले तो, सुबह न आये, रात ही रात चले

how many nights will you
disguise my identity
when you talk about me to your friends?
this separation from me is a long one
and it isn't easy to keep the heart warm
with cold sighs
when will you bridge this gulf between us
must you make this journey from you to me
every single day?

come, slip in stealthily under the sheet of the night
hush—this moon makes quite a noise
come, let's tiptoe behind the clouds
let's burn bit by bit
let's melt drop by drop
may this night stand still—
this half-spent night
come—
quietly pull me in your embrace
under this sheet of the night

under the mellowed winter sun of February
remember—how I would squint my eyes
to steal a look at you
now, in this fading cold
in this soothing warmth of fire
wish we could sing the songs of Mir, softly
in the raga of *marwah*
wish this day does not come to an end
hope the night does not descend
this evening does not set
and if it does, may the morning never come—

तुझ बिन पगली ये पुरवई . . .
तुझ बिन पगली ये पुरवई, आके मेरी चुनरी में भर गई
तू कभी ऐसे ही गले लग जैसे ये पुरवई
आ गले लग जैसे ये पुरवई

साथियां सुन तू
कल जो मुझ को नींद न आये, पास बुला लेना
गोद में अपनी सर रख लेना लोरी सुना देना

चुपके से लग जा गले, रात की चादर तले

let this night stretch on forever
come—quietly pull me in your embrace
under the sheet of the night

crazed by your absence, the easterlies
run into me, billow my *chunari*
sometimes you too fill me up like the easterlies
scoop me in your arms like this wind
listen, my love
if ever sleep forsakes my eyes
reach out to me
cradle my head in your lap
and sing me a lullaby
come—quietly pull me in your embrace
under the sheet of the night

कभी कभी, सुबह सुबह बाथरूम में गुनगुनाई हुई लाईन सारे दिन के लिये गले में अटक जाती है। म्यूज़िक डायरेक्टर शंकर महादेवन के साथ ऐसा ही कुछ हुआ। धुन बनाते हुये ये कच्ची पक्की लाईन उसके गले में अटक गई—'कजरारे कजरारे नैनों वाले . . .' उसके बाद ये डायरेक्टर शाद के गले में पड़ गई। जब मुझ तक आई तो लाईन ऐसी पक चुकी थी कि दोनों पीछे पड़ गये। 'कुछ भी लिखिये, ये लाईन न बदलिये।'

हालांकि कच्चे पक्के मीटर गाते हुये अजीब लाईनें गा जाता है शंकर! 'टूटे न, मेरी टूटे न अंगड़ाई' की जगह उसने गाया था—'चल तू चल मैं जूता पहन के आई।' मैं उससे कुछ पहले ही विशाल के साथ एक गाने में लिख चुका था, 'ओ कजरारे नैनों वाले, नैनां तेरे चम्बल के लूटेरे।' दलेर मेंहदी ने गाया था। लेकिन मेरी सफ़ाई कोई काम न आई। और वो लाईन यही रही।

सिचुएशन एक ढाबे की, जहां ट्रकों के पीछे इस तरह के शेर लिखे रहते हैं—'ज़ालिम नज़र हटाले . . . नज़र मिले जो चौक पर . . .' वग़ैरा—और एक स्ट्रीट सिंगर गाने वाली थी। बाद में सिचुएशन में तबदीली आई और गैस्ट आर्टिस्ट शामिल हुई—ऐश्वर्या राय! बाक़ी तवारीख़ है। ये गाना शादियों पर बैंड बजाने वालों का नेशनल एन्थम बन चुका है। शंकर, शाद मानें न मानें, ये गाना सौ फ़ीसदी ऐश्वर्या की वजह से हिट हुआ है!

ऐसी नज़र से देखा उस ज़ालिम ने चौक पर
हमने कलेजा रख दिया, चाकू की नोक पर

मेरा चैन-वैन सब उजड़ा, ज़ालिम नज़र हटाले
बरबाद हो रहे हैं जी तेरे अपने शहर वाले
आजा, आजा टूटे न अंगड़ाई,
मेरी अंगड़ाई न टूटे, तू आजा . . .

कजरारे कजरारे तेरे कारे कारे नैना
मेरे नैना, मेरे नैना, जुड़वां नैना

सुरमे से लिखे तेरे वादे
आँखों की जबानी आते हैं
मेरे रूमालों पे लब तेरे
बाँध के निशानी जाते हैं

तेरी बातों में क़िमाम की ख़ुशबू है
तेरा आना भी गर्मियों की लू है
आजा, आजा टूटे न अंगड़ाई,
कजरारे कजरारे . . .

आँखों भी कमाल करती हैं
पर्सनल से सवाल करती हैं
पलकों को उठाती भी नहीं
परदे का ख़्याल करती हैं

मेरा ग़म तो किसी से भी छुपता नहीं
दर्द होता है दर्द जब चुभता नहीं

the way that rogue looked at me at the town square
I pinned my heart to the point of a knife, laid my
    feelings bare
ah! my peace is being pillaged
remove your gaze from me, o barbarian—
must you visit ruination upon your own townsfolk
come become one with me
before the stretch of my embrace breaks

(ah! those coal-black, kohl-lined eyes of yours . . .)
yes, what about them . . . what about my twin pools of
    limpid black?

oh! just to think of those promises
you scribbled in the language of your eyes
with the kohl that outlines them
oh! just to think of those assurances
your lips tied on my scarves
oh! just to think of them!

(ah! the intoxicating aroma of *kimam*
that wafts in when you talk
ah! the scorching summer winds
that blaze in when you walk)

come, become one with me
before the stretch of my embrace breaks

आजा, आजा टूटे न अंगड़ाई,
कजरारे कजरारे . . .

तुझसे मिलना पुरानी दिल्ली में
छोड़ आए निशानी दिल्ली में
बल्ली मारां से दरीबे तलक
तेरी मेरी कहानी दिल्ली में

काली कमली वाले को याद कर के
तेरे काले काले नैनों की क़सम खाते हैं
तेरे काले काले नैनों की बलाएं ले लूं
तेरे काले काले नैनों को दुआएं दे दूं

मेरी जान उदास है
होठो पे प्यास है
आजा रे, आजा रे
तेरी बातों में क़िमाम की ख़ुशबू है . . .

आजा, आजा टूटे न अंगड़ाई,
कजरारे कजरारे . . .

oh! look at your eyes pulling off a wonder
probing me with personal questions
without lifting even an eyelash
caring enough for my modesty
and yet tearing me asunder

(ah! but my misery is difficult to hide
ah! the pain you cause when you
stop twisting the thorn in my side
ah! how those kohl-lined coal black eyes
bare their fangs at me

remember—how we met in old Dilli
parts of us still live there
from Ballimaran to Dariba—
all those lanes are strewn with our stories
let *Kali Kamli Walah* be my witness, all I do now is
swear by those remembrances of your coal-black eyes
come let me ward off the evil of those coal-black eyes
come let me whisper a prayer in those twin pools of
    limpid black
look at me beloved, how melancholic I am
come slake the thirst of these lips of mine . . .
come become one with me
before the stretch of my embrace breaks)

come become one with me
before the stretch of my embrace breaks

कभी चांद की तरह टपकी
कभी राह में पड़ी पाई
अठन्नी सी ज़िन्दगी . . . ये ज़िन्दगी

कभी छींक की तरह खनकी
कभी जेब से निकल आई
अठन्नी सी ज़िन्दगी . . . ये ज़िन्दगी

कभी चेहरे पे जड़ी देखी
कहीं मोड़ पर खड़ी देखी
शीशे के मर्तबानों में
दुकान पे पड़ी देखी
अठन्नी सी ज़िन्दगी . . . ये ज़िन्दगी

तमगे़ लगा के मिलती है
मासूमियत से खिलती है
कभी फूल हाथ में लेकर
शाख़ों पे बैठी हिलती है
अठन्नी सी ज़िन्दगी . . . ये ज़िन्दगी

at times it drops like the round moon
at times you find it rolling in the dirt
this half-rupee coin of life

at times it unexpectedly clinks
like a sneeze
at times it slips through your fingers
this half-rupee coin of life

at times you see it stuck in the faces of people
at times you see it standing at the turn of the road
and at others, you find it in glass jars at corner shops
this half-rupee coin of life

you get it with the honour of a medal
it blossoms in all its innocence
and at times you find it with a flower in its hand
swinging from the branch of a tree, beckoning you
this half-rupee coin of life

ऐ ज़िन्दगी गले लगा ले
हमने भी तेरे हर इक ग़म को
गले से लगाया है . . . है ना

हमने बहाने से, छुप के ज़माने से
पलकों के परदे में, घर कर लिया
तेरा सहारा मिल गया है ज़िन्दगी

ऐ ज़िन्दगी गले लगा ले . . .

छोटा सा साया था, आँखों में आया था
हमने दो बूँदों से मन भर लिया
हमको किनारा मिल गया है ज़िन्दगी

ऐ ज़िन्दगी गले लगा ले . . .

come o Life
come—embrace me!
I too have embraced
every little sorrow of yours
haven't I?

and all those moments
in between your sorrows
I stole
on every pretext
from the prying eyes of the world
and found them a home
behind the curtain of my eyelids
I found your support, o Life
now, come—embrace me!

a wayward shadow
of a thought
crosses my eyes
and fills my heart with
just two drops of tears
propelled by those tears
I have come ashore, o Life

come—embrace me!

तुझसे नाराज़ नहीं ज़िंदगी, हैरान हूं मैं
तेरे मासूम सवालों से परेशान हूं मैं

जीने के लिए सोचा ही नहीं, दर्द संभालने होंगे
मुस्कराएं तो मुसकुराने के कर्ज़ उतारने होंगे
मुसकुराऊँ जब भी तो लगता है
जैसे होंठों पे कर्ज़ रखा है

ज़िंदगी तेरे ग़म ने हमें, रिश्ते नए समझाए
मिले जो हमें धूप में मिले, छाँव के ठंडे साए

आज अगर भर आई हैं, बूँदें बरस जाएंगी
कल क्या पता, इनके लिए आँखें तरस जाएंगी
जाने कब गुम हुआ, कहाँ खोया
एक आँसू छुपा के रखा था

तुझसे नाराज़ नहीं ज़िंदगी . . .

74 Masoom (1982)

I am not angry with you, Life
simply baffled
by your innocent questions

never thought that in order to live
I would need to hold on to pain
never thought life would extract
a price for every smile
now—whenever I smile
it feels like these lips are pursed in debt

Life, the trials you threw my way
have taught me relationships anew
the comforts of shade I only found
under the bright scorching sun

today my eyes have welled up with tears
soon they will burst forth, I'm sure
tomorrow, who knows, these sore eyes perhaps
will long for the sight of more—

where have I lost that lone drop of tears
which I had tucked away so safely?

कतरा कतरा मिलती है
कतरा कतरा जीने दो
जिंदगी है, बहने दो
प्यासी हूँ मैं, प्यासी रहने दो

कल भी तो कुछ ऐसा ही हुआ था
नींद में थी, तुमने जब छुआ था
गिरते गिरते बाँहों में, बची मैं
सपने पे पाँव पड़ गया था
सपनों में बहने दो
प्यासी हूँ मैं : . . .

तुमने तो आकाश बिछाया
मेरे नंगे पैरों में ज़र्मी है
पा के भी तुम्हारी आरजू हो
शायद ऐसे जिंदगी हँसी है
आरजू में बहने दो
प्यासी हूँ मैं . . .

हल्के हल्के कोहरे के धुएँ में
शायद आसमाँ तक आ गई हूँ
तेरी दो निगाहों के सहारे
देखो तो कहाँ तक आ गई हूं
कोहरे में बहने दो
प्यासी हूँ मैं . . .

drop by drop it comes to you
drop by drop it has to be lived
that's life—just let it flow
and let my thirst
be unslaked

last night
when you reached out to me
in my sleep—
I tripped on a dream
and nearly stumbled into your arms
let me stay adrift
in my dreams

you laid out
the spread of the sky for me
but my feet are bare, rooted in the earth
I desire you even after attaining you
perhaps that is how life is beautiful
let me stay afloat
in my desire

through the clouds of mist
I have found my way
to the sky, perhaps
holding on to your vision
look how far I have come
let me stay swirling
in this mist
let my thirst
be unslaked

میرا کچھ سامان تمہارے پاس پڑا ہے :

ساون کے کچھ بھیگے بھیگے دن رکھے ہیں

اور میرے اک خط میں لپٹی رات پڑی ہے

وہ رات بجھا دو —

میرا وہ سامان لوٹا دو ....

پتجھڑ ہے کچھ

پتجھڑ میں کچھ پتوں کے گرنے کی آہٹ

کانوں میں اک بار پہن کے لوٹ آئی تھی

پتجھڑ کی وہ شاخ ابھی تک کانپ رہی ہے

وہ شاخ گرا دو —

میرا وہ سامان لوٹا دو ....

ایک اکیلی چھتری میں جب آدھے آدھے بھیگ رہے تھے

آدھے سوکھے آدھے گیلے سوکھا تو میں لے آئی تھی —— گیلا من شاید بستر کے پاس پڑا ہو

The incident attached to this song has become more famous than the song itself by now. When I read this song to Pancham, he thought it was a scene, and appreciated the poetic dialogue. 'It's not a scene,' I said, 'it's a song.'

'Hah!' he reacted, 'you will bring a column from the *Times of India* tomorrow, and ask me to tune it. You are the "limit" yaar.' And he pushed the piece of paper away.

Ashaji smiled. She was present in the music room. A few minutes later, she hummed something under her breath. They were lovely notes and Pancham asked, 'What is that?' She hummed the last phrase of the line '. . . *mujhe lauta do*'. Pancham picked up the piece of paper again, added a few notes and completed the line: '*mera woh saaman mujhe lauta do*'.

Soon he got engrossed in the song and, believe me, he went on to complete the song in that very sitting. The song is a part of history now. Ashaji says she can never finish a concert now without singing this song. The listeners insist.

मेरा कुछ सामान
तुम्हारे पास पड़ा है
सावन के कुछ भीगे भीगे दिन रखे है
और मेरे इक ख़त में लिपटी रात पड़ी है
वो रात बुझा दो . . .
मेरा वो सामान लौटा दो . . .

पतझड़ हैं कुछ !
पतझड़ में कुछ पत्तों के गिरने की आहट
कानों में इक बार पहन कर लौट आई थी
पतझड़ की वो शाख़ अभी तक काँप रही है
वो शाख़ गिरा दो
मेरा वो सामान लौटा दो . . .

एक अकेली छतरी में जब
आधे आधे भीग रहे थे
आधे सूखे, आधे गीले
सूखा तो मैं ले आई थी
गीला मन शायद बिस्तर के पास पड़ा है
वो भिजवा दो . . .

एक सौ सोलह चाँद की रातें . . .
एक तुम्हारे काँधे का तिल . . .
गीली मेहँदी की ख़ुशबू
झूठ मूठ के शिकवे कुछ
झूठ मूठ के वादे भी सब, याद करा दूं
सब भिजवा दो
मेरा वो सामान लौटा दो . . .

a few of my belongings
are still in your possession

a few wet days of monsoon
a night wrapped in a letter
snuff out that night . . .
return to me what is mine

a few autumns
the sound of falling leaves
that I had worn in my ears
that autumn branch is quivering still
bring that branch down . . .
return to me what is mine

once under a single umbrella
when we were both getting half drenched
both of us half wet and half dry
the dry half I had brought along
the wet half, perhaps, is still lying by the bed
send it across . . .

a hundred and sixteen moonlit nights
and that lone mole on your shoulder . . .
the aroma of still-moist henna
a few complaints that were forged
a few false promises too
let me remind you of them all . . .
send them all back to me
return to me what is mine . . .

एक इजाज़त दे दो बस,
जब इसको दफ़नाऊँगी
मैं भी वहीं सो जाऊँगी।

but grant me this one last wish
that when I bury these memories
may I bury myself there too

याद न आए कोई, लहू न रुलाए कोई . . .

अंखियों में बैठा था, अंखियों से उठके
जाने किस देश गया
जोगी मेरा जोगी रे, रांझा, मेरा रांझड़ा
मेरा दरवेश गया, रब्बा

दूर न जाये कोई, याद न आये कोई . . .

शाम के दिये ने आंख भी न खोली
अंधा कर गई रात
जला भी नहीं था देह का बालन
कोयला कर गई रात, रब्बा

और न जलाये कोई, याद न आये कोई . . .

must his memories haunt me
must they extract tears of blood?

suddenly, he stepped out of these eyes
of mine—in which he lived—
and walked away
into the unknown
he—my beloved
my ascetic, my wandering minstrel
where did he go, o Rabba

ah! is there a way to erase his memories
must one's beloved go away this far?

before the evening lamp could open its eyes
the night has blinded me
before this firewood of the body could be lit
the night has charred me into coal

ah! is there a way to stop this burning
to exorcize these memories that extract
tears of blood?

तेरे बिना ज़िंदगी से कोई शिकवा तो नहीं
तेरे बिना ज़िंदगी भी लेकिन ज़िंदगी तो नहीं

काश ऐसा हो तेरे क़दमों से
चुन के मंज़िल चलें, और कहीं, दूर कहीं
तुम अगर साथ हो, मंज़िलों की कमी तो नहीं
तेरे बिना ज़िंदगी से कोई शिकवा तो नहीं

जी में आता है तेरे दामन में
सर छुपाके हम रोते रहें, रोते रहें
तेरी भी आँखों में आँसुओं की नमी तो नहीं
तेरे बिना ज़िंदगी से कोई शिकवा तो नहीं

तुम जो कह दो तो आज की रात
चाँद डूबेगा नहीं, रात को रोक लो
रात की बात है और ज़िंदगी बाकी तो नहीं
तेरे बिना ज़िंदगी से कोई शिकवा तो नहीं

I have no grouse against a life without you
but a life without you is hardly any life

wish we could tread our journey with your steps
pick our destinations afresh and walk
someplace else, someplace far far away—
when you walk along with me
there's no dearth of places to be
and though I have no grouse against a life without you
a life without you is hardly any life

all I wish to do is seek refuge in your *aanchal*
and keep crying; aren't those tears too
that I detect in the moistness of your eyes—
a life without you
is hardly any life

if you say so
the moon will not set tonight
say it—stop this night
it's just the matter of the night
there isn't much left in life
without you
I have no grouse against a life without you
but a life without you is hardly any life

२

७९ गुरू (२००७)

ओ हमदम . . . बिन तेरे क्या जीना
तेरा बिना बे-सुआदी, बे-सुआदी, रतियां
ओ सजना . . .
ओ रूखी रे, रूखी रे
काटूं रे, काटे, कटे नां
तेरे बिना बे-सुआदी, बे-सुआदी, रतियां
ओ सजना . . .

ना जा चाकरी के मारे, न जा
सौतन पुकारे . . . न जा
सावन आयेगा तो,
पूछेगा, न जा रे . . .

फीकी फीकी, बे-सुआदी, बे-सुआदी, रतियां
काटूं रे, काटे न, कटे ना
सजना तेरे बिना काटे कटे ना . . .

तेरे बिना चाँद का सोना, खोटा रे
पीली पीली धूल उड़ावे झूठा रे
तेरे बिना सोना पीतल
तेरे संग कीकर पीपल
आ जा, कटे न रतियां . . .

o breath of my life
how can I live without you?
without you the nights are tasteless
without you these insipid nights
are difficult to while away
however hard I may try

your work pulls you away from me
like another woman competing for your love
must you go—
what will I say to the rain when it asks after you
stay, don't go away

now, these unsavoury tasteless nights
are difficult to while away
without you o friend, o breath of my life

without you this gold of the moon fills up with
    impurities
my search covers me in clouds of yellow dust
without you gold is mere brass
but with you even the thorny shadeless *keekar*
transforms into a shady *peepal*
come now o breath of my life, come
help me savour these tasteless long nights

आज बिछड़े हैं, कल का डर भी नहीं
ज़िंदगी इतनी मुख़्तसर भी नहीं

ज़ख़्म दिखते नहीं अभी लेकिन
ठंडे होंगे तो दर्द निकलेगा
तैश उतरेगा वक़्त का जब भी
चेहरा अंदर से ज़र्द निकलेगा
आज बिछड़े हैं . . .

कहनेवालों का कुछ नहीं जाता
सहनेवाले कमाल करते हैं
कौन ढूँढ़े जवाब दर्दों के
लोग तो बस सवाल करते हैं
आज बिछड़े हैं . . .

कल जो आएगा जाने क्या होगा
बीत जाएँ जो कल नहीं आते
वक़्त की शाख़ तोड़ने वालों
टूटी शाख़ों पे फल नहीं आते
आज बिछड़े हैं . . .

कच्ची मिट्टी है, दिल भी, इन्सां भी
देखने ही में सख़्त लगता है
आँसू पोंछे तो आँसुओं के निशाँ
ख़ुश्क होने में वक़्त लगता है

आज बिछड़े हैं, कल का डर भी नहीं
ज़िंदगी इतनी मुख़्तसर भी नहीं

we may've separated today
but life is not that short
that we may not meet tomorrow

the wounds are not visible, not yet
but when the wounds begin to heal
the pain—inevitable—will come
when the anger of time cools off
the face within will emerge blanched

tattlers stay unscathed
but the tenacity of those who
bear the brunt is commendable
people only pose questions
in perverse pleasure
for no one is really interested
in knowing your pain

we may've separated today
but life is not that short
that we may not meet tomorrow
but whatever the day to come may bring
it will never be the day that has gone by
those who saw off the branch of time
forget that sawed-off branches never blossom

this human heart, this human body
may look strong, robust
but made of dust, it crumbles to the touch
wipe the tears whichever way you will
it still takes a lifetime
for the stains to dry

we may've separated today
but life is not that short
that we may not meet tomorrow

Dil hoom hoom kare

The heart makes many a demand, but only one sound: 'dhak-dhak'. Be it the heart of Madhuri Dixit, or of Shammi Kapoor. The language has kept changing with the times but the heart's sound has always remained the same in our film songs. Particularly Hindi film songs.

Suddenly I came across this Assamese folk song where the sound the heart makes is described as 'hoom-hoom'. I just loved it. It is much more romantic than 'dhak-dhak'. There were some apprehensions but I insisted on using the phrase 'hoom-hoom' in this song, since the entire tune was based on the same Assamese folk song, only the lines changed according to the situation.

दिल हुम हुम करे घबराए
घन धम धम करे गरजाए
इक बूंद कभी पानी की
मोरी अंखियों से बरसाए

तेरी झोरी डारूं
सब सूखे पात जो लागे
तेरा छुआ लागे
मोरी सूखी डाल हरियाए

जिस तन को छुआ तूने
उस तन को छुपाऊं
जिस मन को लागे नैना
वो किस को दिखाऊं

ओ मोरे चंद्रमा
तेरी चांदनी अंग जलाए
तेरी ऊंची है अटारी
मैंने पंख लिए कटवाए

दिल हुम हुम करे घबड़ाए

81 Rudaali (1993)

the heart rumbles and mumbles
dark clouds of worries roar and thunder
and yet I keep yearning
for even a single drop of tears
to burst forth from my eyes

I know your touch can sprout life
in these shrivelled stumps of my existence
and in this hope I gather and preserve
all the wilted leaves of my life

your love
that has touched my body
is difficult to hide
but your touch
that has impinged itself on my soul—
how do I bare it to you?

you are my moon, and yet
your soothing rays scorch my skin
your perch is high
and my wings freshly clipped

the heart rumbles and mumbles . . .

मेरे पी को पवन किस गली ले चली
कोई रोको, मेरी ज़िंदगी ले चली

वक़्त बीजा था, बोया था, उसके लिए
मैंने पल पल पिरोया था उसके लिए
मेरे दिन रात की रौशनी ले चली
मेरे पी को . . . .

ज़हर है रात, हर रात, पर जीना है
एक वादे की ख़ैरात पर जीना है
मेरे होंठों पे थी जो हंसी ले चली
मेरी पी को . . .

मुझसे रूठी, कहीं और ये जुड़ गई
ज़िंदगी अजनबी रास्ता मुड़ गई
एक उम्मीद थी, आख़िरी, ले चली
मेरे पी को . . .

where is this wind taking my beloved
stop this wind, someone, it's carrying my life away

I had seeded time, harvested
the sprouts of time, for him
strung the beads of moments
together, for him
and now the wind's carrying
the light of my days and nights
carrying it all away

the night's a miasma—every night
shooting its poison into me, but
I have to live
live on the largesse
of a single promise
and the wind's blowing
the smile that was on my lips
blowing it all away

life's squabbled with me
and taken up a new lover
suddenly swerved along that
strange bend in the road
into the unknown
and the wind's blowing
that lone last hope
blowing it all away

जाने क्या सोच कर नहीं गुज़रा
एक पल रात भर नहीं गुज़रा

अपनी तन्हाई का औरों से न शिकवा करना
तुम अकेले ही नहीं हो, सभी अकेले हैं
यह अकेला सफ़र नहीं गुज़रा
जाने क्या सोच कर नहीं गुज़रा . . .

दो घड़ी जीने की मोहलत तो मिली है सबको
तुम भी मिल जाओ घड़ी भर को, यह कम होता है
इक घड़ी का सफ़र नहीं गुज़रा
जाने क्या सोच कर नहीं गुज़रा . . .
एक पल रात भर नहीं गुज़रा . . .

83 Kinara (2007)

I don't know why
that one lone moment
refused to pass by
the entire length of the night

this lonesome journey
never ends—
do not bemoan
your loneliness to others:
you are not the only one

a two-moment is all
that we are given to live—
the moment in which
I am with you
fleets by
but the other—
the one without you
is the one that refuses to pass by—
I don't know why

पूछे जो कोई मेरी निशानी
रंग हिना लिखना
गोरे बदन पे उंगली से मेरा
नाम अदा लिखना

कभी कभी आस पास चांद रहता है
कभी कभी आस पास शाम रहती है

आऊं तो सुबह, जाऊं तो मेरा
नाम सबा लिखना
बर्फ़ पड़े तो बर्फ़ पे मेरा
नाम दुआ लिखना

ज़रा ज़रा आग वाग पास रहती है
ज़रा ज़रा कांगड़ी की आंच रहती है

जब तुम हंसते हो दिन हो जाता है
तुम गले लगा लो तो दिन सो जाता है

डोली उठाए आएगा दिन तो
पास बिठा लेना
कल जो मिले तो माथे पे मेरे
सूरज उगा देना

कभी कभी आस पास धूप रहेगी
कभी कभी आस पास रंग रहेंगे

पूछे जो कोई मेरी निशानी
रंग हिना लिखना!

if they ask you my identity, say—
I am the colour of henna
as traced by your fingertips on my fair body
I am spelt grace

tell them the moon hovers around me at times
and at times I am wrapped in the dusk of the evening
write down my name as morning when I arrive
put it down as night when I leave
and when the snowflakes begin to fall
scribble my name on the fallen snow as prayer
tell them, there's the blaze of fire about her
and at times, the comforting glow of the *kangri*

when you laugh, the day fills up with sunshine
and when you embrace me, the day lulls itself to sleep

and when the day comes as a newly-wed in a palanquin
take my hand and make me sit next to you
and if you find tomorrow
make it sprout the sun from my forehead

if they ask you my identity, say—
I am henna
tell them the sun shines around me at times
and at times I'm enveloped in colours of myriad hues

जिनके सर हो इश्क़ की छांव
पांव के नीचे जन्नत होगी
चल छैंया छैंया छैंया . . .
सर इश्क़ की छांव, चल छैंया छैंया
पांव जन्नत चले, चल छैंया छैंया

वो यार है जो ख़ुशबू की तरह
है जिसकी जुबां उर्दू की तरह
मेरी शाम रात, मेरी कायनात
वो यार मेरा, सैंया सैंया
चल छैंया छैंया . . .

गुलपोश कभी इतराए कहीं
महके तो नज़र आ जाए कहीं
तावीज़ बना के पहनूं उसे
आयत की तरह मिल जाए कहीं

मेरा नग़्मा वही, मेरा कलमा वही
वो यार मिसाले ओस चले
पांव के तले फ़िरदौस चले
कभी डाल डाल
कभी पात पात
मैं हवा पे ढूंढूं उस के निशां
चल छैंया छैंया . . .

those who walk in the shade of love
must have paradise under their feet
keep walking in the shade of love

the companion who walks along
like fragrance
and whispers in a mellifluous tongue
is my dusk, is my night
the centre of my evolution
my beloved, my refuge in love

keep walking in the shade of love

conceals himself in flowers
reveals himself in fragrance
my companion—
if I were to find him like an *ayat*
I would wear him
like a charm around my neck

keep walking in the shade of love

he is my song of celebration
he is my hymn of faith
he moves like dewdrops
with paradise under his feet
stepping over the branches
stepping on the leaves
and I'm looking for his presence
in the breeze

keep walking in the shade of love

मैं उस के रूप का शैदाई
वो धूप छांव सा हरजाई
वो शोख़ है रंग बदलता है
मैं रंग रूप का सौदाई
चल छैंया छैंया . . .

I am a lover of his forms
he flits between shadow and light
mischievous is he, changes his colour
and a seeker I am of his colours and forms

keep walking in the shade of love

Jaane do mujhe, jaane do

Dil Padosi Hai was recorded in a semi-professional studio of HMV's on Phirozeshah Mehta Road, in the late hours of night so as to avoid the day's traffic noise. At that time today's electronic equipments didn't exist at all. But listen to the rich sounds of music created by Pancham (polluted by remixes in recent times).

After finishing his professionally assigned work in the music room, he would shift to my place, saying, 'चल अब फ़ालतू काम तेरे घर पे करेंगे।' Accompanied by Ashaji, we would continue work on the album.

We were keen to make songs that were really different from the film situations. Some situations are those of extramarital relationships.

> रात क्रिसमस की थी।
> न तेरे बस की थी,
> न मेरे बस की थी।

In this particular song there is the pleading of a wife whose husband beats her up. She still loves him but wants to part from him. She can only plead:

> जाने दो मुझे, जाने दो।

जाने दो मुझे, जाने दो
रंजिशें या गिले, वफ़ा के सिले
जो गए जाने दो
जाने दो मुझे, जाने दो

थोड़ी ख़लिश होगी
थोड़ा-सा ग़म होगा
तन्हाई तो होगी
एहसास कम होगा
गहरी ख़राशों की
गहरी निशानियाँ हैं
चेहरे के नीचे कितनी
सारी कहानियाँ हैं
माज़ी के सिलसिले
जा चुके, जाने दो

उम्मीदो-शौक़ सारे, लौटा रही हूँ मैं
रुसवाई थोड़ी-सी, ले जा रही हूँ मैं
बासी दिलासों की, शब तो गुज़ार आए
आँखों से गर्द सारी, रो के उतार आए
आँखों के बुलबुले बह गए
जाने दो
जाने दो मुझे . . .

let go of me
there's nothing left to hold on to—
the agony and the accusations
loyalty and its atonements
all those are now gone
now, let go of me

there will be
a little discomfort, a little distress
an overwhelming loneliness
but you will not feel much pain—
each scar on my face
has a tale to tell
but must we parade the cortege of the past
let the past stay in the past
now, just let go of me

your vows and your commitments
I am returning to you
my honour
—that you fragmented—
is all that I am taking with me
the night of stale promises
I have already lived through
the illusions in the eyes
I have already cast off in tears
the bubbles in the eyes
are all washed away

all those are now gone
now, let go of me

इतना लम्बा कश लो यारो, दम निकल जाए
ज़िंदगी सुलगाओ यारो, ग़म निकल जाए
यारो . . .

दिल में कुछ जलता है शायद, धुँआ धुँआ सा लगता है
आँख में कुछ चुभता है शायद, सपना कोई सुलगता है
दिल फूंकों और इतना फूंकों, दर्द पिघल जाए
ज़िंदगी सुलगाओ यारो . . . यारो . . .

तेरे साथ गुज़ारी रातें गर्म गर्म सी लगती हैं
सब रातें रेशम की नहीं, पर नर्म नर्म सी लगती हैं
रात ज़रा करवट बदलो तो बल निकल जाए
यारो . . .

इतना लम्बा कश लो यारो, दम निकल जाए
ज़िंदगी सुलगाओ यारो . . . यारो . . .

take such a deep drag at life, o friends
that its breath's sucked out
light up your lives, o friends
so that your sorrow's smoked out

something's burning in the heart, perhaps
it appears all smoky
something's stinging in the eye
perhaps it's a dream smouldering
burn your heart, and burn it so well
that your pain melts away

the nights spent with you
appear warm, still
and though all nights
are not silken, yet
they feel soft and tender
so soft that when
the night turns on its side
the disc of life slips

फूंक दे . . .
पीले पीले से जंगल में बहता धुआं
घूंट घूंट जल रहा हूं, पी रहा हूं पत्तियां
आंखें हैं धुआं धुआं, नम हैं सारी बत्तियां
आस पास कुछ नहीं, जी उदास है बड़ा
दर्द सब्ज़ हैं अभी, मुझको रास है बड़ा
फूंक दे . . .

हयात फूंक दे, हवास फूंक दे
सांसों से सिला हुआ लिबास फूंक दे

सर चढ़ी है ख़ुमारी और ज़मीन डोलती है
बे-ज़ुबान दास्तां रात भर बोलती है
लब पे जल रही है जो बात, फूंक दे
होंटों से लिपटी ये रात फूंक दे
होंटों से रात की राख फूंक दे . . .

जब नशा टूटता है, कितने टुकड़े गिरे हैं
होश चुनने लगे हम, हम भी क्या सरफिरे हैं
लब पे जल रही है जो बात, फूंक दे . . .
फूंक दे . . .

puff in—
the billowing smoke in the jaundiced jungle
the smouldering yellowed leaves
and burn—
bit by bit

the eyes are all smoky
and the lights all dim
with nothing to hold on to
a sadness seeps in
and you tend to like the pain—
that still lingers

blow, blow it all up—
in smoke:
the life
the consciousness
and the ensemble that you have
threaded together with breath

the intoxication gets to your head
the ground beneath your feet sways
and voiceless tales prattle all night

the silence smouldering on your lips, smoke it out
the night wrapped around your lips, smoke it out
and the ash of the burnt night, smoke it out

the inebriation shatters
falling around you in fragments
are you insane to wish—
for sobriety?

कच्चे रंग उतर जाने दो
मौसम है, गुज़र जाने दो

नदी में इतना है पानी
सब धुल जाएगा
मट्टी का ढेला है
ये घुल जाएगा

इतनी सी मिट्टी है
नदियों को बहना है
नदियों को बहने दो
सारे रंग बिखर जाने दो

कच्चे रंग उतर जाने दो . . .

शीशम के पत्तों पे पानी
बूंद बूंद बजता रहता है
बारिश बीत भी जाए तो
देर तलक टपका रहता है

बूंदों से भिगो देना
बारिशों की आदत थी
बारिशों की आदत है
ये बौछार गुज़र जाने दो

कच्चे रंग उतर जाने दो . . .

these colours are not fast
let them bleed away
it's just another season
let it weather away

the river runs deep, holds enough water
to wash away the paint, all the taint
purged of your colours, you are a lump of clay
the water runs deep and the river is
your perfect refuge

the river carries millions of tons of sediment
your handful of dirt will not change its course
come, step in it—let it run your colours away

the rain pitter-patters a tune
on the leaves of *shisham*
and the melody of that song
still drips from the leaves
even when the rain's gone

it was the wont of the rain
to soak you in its showers
and it still is—let this
cloudburst weather away

उड़ते हुए सूखे तिनकों का
जोड़ना और पिरोना क्या
अन्धे गुलों का शाखों पे,
होना और न होना क्या

रंग बदल लेना,
मौसमों की आदत थी
मौसमों की आदत है
शाख़ें ख़ाली कर जाने दो . . .

कच्चे रंग उतर जाने दो . . .

dry twigs blowing in the wind
do not bend into a weave—
must you then gather them?
must blind buds
cling on to a branch?

it was the wont of the seasons
to change colours and
it still is—let the seasons
shake the leaves off the trees

let these colours bleed away

पानी, पानी रे, खारे पानी रे
नैनों में भर जा, नींदें ख़ाली कर जा . . .

पानी पानी इन पहाड़ों की ढलानों से उतर जाना
धुँआ धुँआ कुछ वादियाँ भी आएँगी, गुज़र जाना
इक गाँव आएगा, मेरा घर आएगा
जा मेरे घर जा, नींदें ख़ाली कर जा

ये रूदाली जैसी रातें जगरातों में बिता देना
मेरी आंखों मे जो बोले मीठे पाखी तो उड़ा देना
बर्फ़ों में लगे मौसम पिघले, मौसम हरे कर जा

पानी, पानी रे, खारे पानी रे
नैनों में भर जा, नींदें ख़ाली कर जा . . .

rain—come
become a little tainted
a little saline
come, rain in my eyes
flush out all the sleep
and roll . . .

roll down the slopes of these mountains
to the foot of the hills
you will come across a few valleys
enveloped in mist
no . . . do not stop there . . .
when you roll down a little further
you will come across a village
you will come across my home
stacked in that home of mine
you will find all my cast-off sleep—
flood into my home
flush out all the sleep

calm the sounds of the night
the dirge of separation
stay awake, on guard
shoo away the songbirds of desire
that may roost in these eyes, but . . .

but the snow that trapped the seasons of love
has begun to melt
let those pale frozen leaves
turn green

rain—come
become a little tainted
a little saline
come flood in my eyes, flush out all the sleep

I have written many a poem on death. It's something you cannot experience yourself in life; I have tried to experience it through others. For *Anand*, I wrote a poem to that effect for the character of Anand:

मुझ से इक नज़्म (कविता) का वादा है मिलेगी मुझ को !

But this is one of my favourite songs, written on the death of a friend.

न ले के जाओ, मेरे दोस्त का जनाज़ा है
अभी तो गर्म है मिट्टी, ये जिस्म ताज़ा है

उलझ गई है कहीं सांस खोल दो इसकी
लबों पे आई है जो बात पूरी करने दो
अभी उम्मीद भी ज़िन्दा है, दर्द ताज़ा है
न ले के जाओ . . .

जगाओ इसको, गले मिलके अलविदा तो कहूं
ये कैसी रूख़सती है ये, क्या सलीक़ा है
अभी तो सीने का हर एक ज़ख़्म ताज़ा है
न ले के जाओ . . .

stop, o pall-bearers
desist!
he's my friend—
you can't take him just yet!
feel! the body's still warm

look—his lips are still quivering
hearken, he's saying something
the hope's still alive
the pain's still raw
the wound's still pulsating
the breath's being strangled even now—
unshroud him!

wake him—
I need to hug him goodbye

stop, o pall-bearers
desist!

जागो जागो जागते रहो, जागो जागो जागते रहो
रातों का हमला है
मकड़ी के जाले हैं, अंधेरे पाले हैं, चंद लोगों ने!
जागो जागो जागते रहो . . .

आग के दांतों में ईमान फंसे हैं
आग के दांतों में इनसान फंसे हैं
आग जब भौंकती है
डर लगता है
आदमी छौंकती है
डर लगता है
इनसान की नसलों को, पैरों में रौंदा है, चंद लोगों ने!
जागो जागो जागते रहो . . .

फिर गिरी गर्दन, सर कटने लगे हैं
लोग बंटते ही, ख़ुदा बंटने लगे हैं
नाम जो पूछे कोई
डर लगता है
किस को पूजे कोई
डर लगता है
कितनी बार मुझे सूली पे टांगा है, चंद लोगों ने!
जागो जागो जागते रहो!

rise! awaken! stay awake!
this is the invasion of the nights
the onslaught of their spidery tentacles
a handful of men breeding darkness—
rise! awaken! stay awake!

in the jaws of fire honesty is snared
in the jaws of fire people are snared
when the fire snarls—
we are scared
this fire fries people—
we are scared
a handful of men have trampled
the race of humans under their feet
rise! awaken! stay awake!

once again necks are being chopped
once again heads are rolling
the moment people split, God is splintered
when someone asks our name—
we are scared
which God should we kneel to—
we are scared

how often has a handful of men
hung me from the scaffold—
rise! awaken! stay awake!

वतना वे, ओ मेरे यार वतना वे

बट गए तेरे आंगन
बुझ गए चूल्हे सांझे
लुट गई तेरी हीरें
मर गए तेरे रांझे

कौन तुझे पानी पूछेगा, फ़सलें सींचेगा
कौन तेरी माटी में ठन्डी छांव बीजेगा

बैरी काट के ले गए तेरियां ठंडिया छांवा वे

हम ना रहे तो कौन बसाएगा तेरा वीराना
मुड़ के हम ना देखेंगे और तू भी याद न आना
गिट्टे कंच्चे बांट के कर ली कट्टी, वतना वे

बट गए तेरे आंगन
बुझ गए चूल्हे सांझे
वतना वे!

o my motherland! my beloved motherland!

your patios divided
your hearths extinguished
your lasses defiled
your gallants killed

with us not around
who'll look after you
who'll water your crops
who will tame your wilderness
who'll sow cool shades
in your earth?

the pillaging enemy
has chopped up and carried off
your comforting genteel shades

the marbles
and the stones of hopscotch
from our last games together
you have thrown at our faces
and so easily
severed all
childhood ties of friendship

ये रात . . .ये रात
झिल्ली सी छिपकली रात
कौड़ीयाले कोबरे की रात
न उगली ही जाए, ना निगली ही जाए
ये काली ज़हरीली रात

पल पल बल खाती
बल बल उलझाती
पलकें झपकती, ये रात

सन्नाटे की सेज पे सोई
सांप सी सरकती रात

वीराना वीराना है वीराना
दिल को लाख बसाले ये दीवाना
उजड़े उजड़े रहते हैं दिल सारे,
वीरानों से बसता है वीराना

संटी से मारती है
फुंकारती है,
काली, कौड़ीयाली रात

आबी आबी रात बड़ी तेज़ाबी
गिर न ना जाए हाथ से चांद रकाबी
डूब रहे हैं सारे कूल किनारे
उमड़ उमड़ के रात आई सैलाबी

this night—
this thin film of a reptilian night
clings onto you
and you can neither spit nor swallow
the venom of this black night
this spotted cobra of a night—

this squinting, blinking night—
contorts itself ever so often
and with each twist
coils you tighter in its embrace

this night
sleeps on a bed of dour silence
and creeps on you like a serpent

the heart is a forsaken wasteland
however hard this lovelorn lunatic
may try to restore it, it will stay
forever a barren badland—
wilderness yields only to more wilderness

it hisses—
whiplashes with its forked tongue
this black, spotted night

this river of the night is acidic
and I fear, lest the saucer of the moon
slips off my hand—
it corrodes through the shores and the sands

खौलते बदन पर,
बोलते बदन पर
जलती उबलती रात

ये रात . . .
झिल्ली सी छिपकली रात . . .

the way this howling, tempestuous night descends
on this boiling body
on this babbling body
this burning, sizzling night

this night
this thin film of a reptilian night

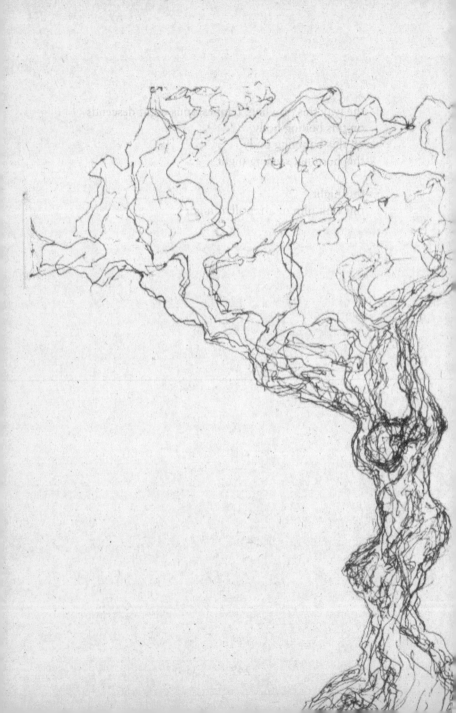

वो बंगाली ज़बान हो, मिठाई, शायरी हो, या . . .! मैंने बंगाली लड़की से शादी की है। मेरे गुरू टैगोर है। दूसरे गुरू बिमल राय जिन की वजह से मैं फ़िल्मों में दाख़िल हुआ। उनकी फ़िल्म 'बंदनी' में पहला गाना लिख कर—'मोरा गोरा अंग लई ले!'

बंगाली बोलना बहुत अच्छा लगता है। 'लव लैटर्स' लिख लिख कर पढ़ने लिखने की प्रैक्टिस की थी। कवितायें भी लिखीं, पर पहली बार किसी ने बंगाली फ़िल्म के लिये गाने लिखने के लिये कहा। कुल तीन गाने थे। दो सन्जीदा से गाने तो मैंने लिख लिये, लेकिन तीसरा धौल धप्पा जैसा नहीं लिख पाया। वो सपन चक्रवर्ती ने लिखा। तब लगा था काश बंगाली भी मेरी मादरी ज़बान होती तो क्या मज़ा आता। ज़मीन पर रोड़े मिट्टी में उगी मादरी ज़बान का मज़ा ही कुछ और होता है।

घूम थेके उठ लो जे
चांद एक माझ आकाशे
ऑबाक होएछे देखे
तारा नेई आशेपाशे

गोभीर निशिते चांद
ऍका ऍका जाबे कोथाये
हारानो तारा ऍखोन
ऑन्धोकारे पाबे कोथाये
ऑधारे सागोरे कार जैनो
गाॅन्थो भाशे
घूम थेके उठलो जे चांद . . .

रातेर शेषे जोदि
पाये ना शे निजेर ठिकाना
चाॅद आर उठबे ना,
छेड़े जाबे आकाशखाना
केउ जोदि डाक दिये
ए साॅमोय फिरे आशे
घूम थेके उठलो जे चांद . . .

the moon wakes up
from his slumber
confounded by his loneliness
in the dark stretch of the sky
the stars, nowhere in sight

the moon wanders alone, rummaging
the vast expanse of the night sky
but the search fatigues him
and the moon begins to sink
in his own loneliness

whose fragrance is this
that lingers in this sea of darkness?

if by the end of the night
the moon does not find
the stars, he will
not rise—never again
heart-broken he will
desert the skyscape

if, only if
somebody could come back and
call out to him now

मादरी ज़बान का आराम बड़ा कमाल होता है। आदमी नंगे पांव ही घर आंगन में घूमता रहता है। हर दिन इतबार का दिन लगता है। तैयार होके नहीं बैठना पड़ता। पंजाबी में ये गाना लिखते हुये बिल्कुल ऐसा ही महसूस हुआ। लफ़्ज़ों की तलाश नहीं करनी पड़ी। मुझे खुद ख़बर नहीं थी कि मेरे अन्दर इस क़दर पंजाबी बीजी हुई है। जब लिखने बैठा तो अपने आप ही ढोलक की थाप सुनाई देने लगी। और फिर भूपी (भूपेन्द्र) जिसके अंग अंग में पंजाबी का लहजा बसा हुआ है, उसने कमाल गाया!

हम दोनों ने बंगालनों से शादी की है। मुझ पर तो फिर भी कुछ असर हुआ, वो तो बिल्कुल चिकना घड़ा है। पूरा पंजाबी!

सोने विच मढ़के
मंतर पढ़ के
लभ के तवीत ल्यावे नी
फड़ फड़ गले च पावे नी
ते नाले पावें झप्पियां
पखियां वे पखियां . . .

पखियां वे पखियां
पखियां वे पखियां
पखियां वे पखियां
प्याज कटाइयां चिट्ठी आवे
भर जान अखियां
पखियां वे पखियां . . .

लभया फिरे मुंडा बारीयां दे ओले
चिट्ठियां छुपावां ते ओ बगलां टटोले
होकयां य लुकियां ने
हिक विच रखियां
पखियां वे पखियां . . .

पखियां वे पखियां
पखियां वे पखियां
पखियां वे पखियां
प्याज कटाइयां चिट्ठी आवे
भर जान अखियां
पखियां वे पखियां . . .

he spells a charm
into the amulet
gilds it in gold
and seeks me out
to tie it around my neck
but friends, that's just an excuse
to hold me in his embrace

(hear . . . hear . . .
a confession at last . . .
look how she blushes, perspires
bring out the palm-leaf fans . . .
cool her down . . .)

I seek out work in the kitchen
chop onions that make me cry
but that's just an excuse
to hide the tears that
the tender words of his love-letter brings

(hear . . . hear . . .
a confession at last
bring out the palm-leaf fans)

he pulls me behind the window
to look for that letter
for that admission of his love
but I tuck it in my bosom
and give him an excuse
to search me . . .

सावे सावे तेड़ा पीछे करदि ऊड़ीका
सप सप बोल के मारियां छींका
खसमा नु खानियां भेड़ियां
पखियां वे पखियां . . .

पखियां वे पखियां
पखियां वे पखियां
पखियां वे पखियां
प्याज कटाइयां चिट्ठी आवे
भर जान अखियां
पखियां वे पखियां . . .

(hear . . . hear . . .
a confession at last
bring out the palm-leaf fans . . .)

I secretly wait for him
behind the green trees
when the shout of 'snake! snake!'
makes me jump out of my hiding place—
hear . . . hear . . . rogue friends of mine
bring out the palm-leaf fans . . .

कभी पास बैठो किसी फूल के पास
सुनो जब महकता है
बहुत कुछ ये कहता है
कभी गुनगुना के, कभी मुस्करा के
कभी चुपके-चुपके
कभी खिलखिला के
जहाँ पे सवेरा हो
बसेरा वहीं है

कभी छोटे-छोटे
शबनम के क़तरे
देखे तो होंगे, सुबह-ओ-सवेरे
ये नन्ही-सी आँखें, जागी हैं शब-भर
बहुत कुछ है दिल में
बस इतना है लब पर
जहाँ पे सवेरा हो
बसेरा वहीं है

ना मिट्टी ना गारा, ना सोना सजाना
जहाँ प्यार देखो वहीं घर बनाना
ये दिल की इमारत बनती है दिल से
दिलासों को छू के, उम्मीदों से मिल के
जहाँ पे सवेरा हो
जहाँ पे बसेरा हो
सवेरा वहीं है

sometimes sit by a flower
there's a lot it says when it blooms
listen to its hum, to its smile
to its whisper, to its chuckle
what it says is—
where the dawn comes
that's where I make my home

you must have seen
the tiny little drops of dew
in the mornings
those small little eyes
that have stayed up all night
they have a lot in their hearts
but only this on their lips—
where the dawn comes
that's where we make our home

look for neither mud nor mortar
neither gold nor adornment
build your home where you find love
for the home is built by the heart
at the confluence of hopes
on the touch of promises
where the home is
that's where the dawn comes

थोड़ी-सी ज़मीं, थोड़ा आसमाँ
तिनकों का बस इक आशियाँ

माँगा है जो तुमसे, वह ज़्यादा तो नहीं है
देने को तो जाँ दे दें, वादा तो नहीं है
कोई तेरे वादे पे जीता है कहाँ
थोड़ी-सी ज़मीं . . .

मेरे घर के आँगन में छोटा-सा झूला हो
सौंधी-सौंधी मिट्टी होगी, लेपा हुआ चूल्हा हो
थोड़ी-थोड़ी आग होगी, थोड़ा-सा धुआँ
थोड़ी-सी ज़मीं . . .

रात कट जाएगी तो कैसे दिन बिताएँगे
बाजरे के खेतों में कौए उड़ाएँगे
बाजरे के सिट्टों-जैसे बेटे हों जवाँ
थोड़ी-सी ज़मीं, थोड़ा आसमाँ
तिनकों का बस इक आशियाँ

98 Sitara (1980)

a small little piece of the earth
a patch of the sky
and just a nest of twigs—
what I ask of you isn't much, is it?

I could solemnly swear you my life
but that's one promise that you do not seek
can one bank on your tall promises
all I ask of you is
a small little piece of the earth
a patch of the sky
and just a nest of twigs

I promise you
a pretty little swing in the courtyard of my house
the scent of the earth
the aroma wafting from the earthen oven
a little fire
and a little smoke
a small little piece of the earth
a patch of sky

the night will pass, but how are we to spend the day
we will chase the crows away in the fields of millet
may our sons grow up like these golden stalks of millet
a small little piece of the earth
a patch of sky
are all that we ask for

दिल ढूंढता है फिर वही फुर्सत के रात दिन
बैठे रहें तसव्वुरे जानां किए हुए

जाड़ों की नर्म धूप और आंगन में लेट कर
आंखों पें खींच कर तेरे आँचल के साए को
औन्धे पड़े रहें, कभी कर्वट लिए हुए

या गर्मियों की रात जो पुरवाइयां चलें
ठन्डी सफ़ेद चादरों पे जागें देर तक
तारों को देखते रहें, छत पर पड़े हुए

बर्फ़ीली सर्दियों में किसी भी पहाड़ पर
वादी में गूंजती हुई ख़ामोशियां सुने
आंखों में भीगे भीगे से लम्हे लिए हुए

दिल ढूँढता है, फिर वही . . .

the heart yearns, yet again
for those carefree days and nights
when we would laze about
wallowing in thoughts of the beloved

put my head in your lap
in some sunny corner of the courtyard
tug at the corner of your *aanchal*
pull it over my squinting eyes
and bask under the soothing winter sun
and lie—oblivious to the world—forever

stay up the summer nights on the roof
lie on cool snowy sheets
the easterlies caressing our faces—
deciphering patterns in the stars
till they fade away

in freezing winter, motionless
perched atop a mountain peak
listen to our silence echo
against the valley walls
the moments wet with mist in our eyes

the heart yearns once again . . .

आजा आजा, जिन्दे, शमियाने के तले
आजा ज़री वाले, नीले आसमान के तले
जय हो!

रत्ती रत्ती, सच्ची, मैंने जान गंवाई है
नच नच कोयलों पे, रात बिताई है

अखियों की नींद मैंने फूंकों से उड़ा दी
गिन गिन तारे मैंने उंगली जलाई है

आजा आजा, जिन्दे, शमियाने के तले
आजा ज़री वाले, नीले आसमान के तले
जय हो!

चख ले, हां, चख ले
ये रात शहद है, चख ले
रख ले, हां दिल है
दिल आख़री हद है, रख ले

काला-काला काजल तेरा
कोई काला-जादू है ना

आजा आजा, जिन्दे, शमियाने के तले
आजा ज़री वाले, नीले आसमान के तले
जय हो!

come, come o beloved
come step with me under this canopy
this azure canopy of a sky
filigreed with the light of the stars

jai ho!

believe you me—
each night, I saw
life drain out of me
drop by drop
each night I danced away
on a bed of burning coals
I blew away sleep from my eyes
my fingertips singed
from counting stars all night

come, come o beloved
come step with me under this canopy
this azure canopy of a sky
filigreed with the light of the stars

jai ho!

but tonight—
this night is a pot of honey
come let's savour it
and keep this heart of mine
with you, for the heart is
the last frontier

कब से, हां, कब से
जो लब पे रुकी है, कह दे
कह दे, हां, कह दे
अब आंख झुकी है, कह दे

थम के, हां, थम के
शब तेज़ क़दम है, दम ले
दम ले, हां, दम ले
कुछ वक़्त भी कम है, दम ले

ऐसी–ऐसी रौशन आंखें
रौशन दो दो हीरे हैं क्या?

आजा आजा, ज़िन्दे, शमियाने के तले
आजा ज़री वाले, नीले आसमान के तले
जय हो!

look! I am under your spell
that black kohl in your eyes
has whipped up
a kind of black magic

come, come o beloved
come step with me under this canopy
this azure canopy of a sky
filigreed with the light of the stars

jai ho!

come, say out those words
that you have always
pulled back from your lips
look at you—
blushing, lowering your eyes
it is now or never
come, say it

but let's pause—
this night is fleet-footed
let's take a breather
let's prolong this night
but your eyes
with their brilliance of diamonds
have already lit up the night sky
filigreed it with the light of the stars

come, come o beloved
come step with me under this canopy
this azure canopy of a sky
filigreed with the light of the stars

jai ho!

Jai ho

This song is history by now.
As the idiom goes, history must repeat itself.
The first time it brought an Oscar for me.
The second time . . .

अब और क्या कहें?

Index of First Lines

Index of Albums

*Non-film Album

*Non-film Album

For Pali of Pali Hill—
He was with me till the end of this book.
When I finished the last page and mailed it, he breathed his last.